THE SUBCONTRACTOR'S EDGE

BOOST YOUR MARGINS AND CASHFLOW, AND END CONSTRUCTION'S BOOM-BUST CYCLE

CIAN BRENNAN

⚠️ **WARNING**
FOR CONSTRUCTION SUBCONTRACTORS ONLY

What others have said

'I would highly recommend this book to any contractor who knows they have the practical skills but feels lost when it comes to understanding the business side.'

Corey Branks – Techsteel Prefabricated Framing Systems

'This book is a game-changer. I felt confident with a solid, straightforward strategy that's easy to follow. No fluff – just practical, actionable advice that's simple but effective in a hectic industry.'

Brendan Carey – Lee Group

'Any business in construction will benefit from reading this book. *The Subcontractor's Edge* pinpoints the biggest issues construction contractors have faced over the past decade.'

Kelvin Andrijich – Alltype Engineering

'I've been looking for a book like this for a long, long time. The roadmap is simple yet insightful, showing how to scale effectively and achieve long-term success.'

Prometheus Siddiqui – Brockman Engineering

Foundational principle

Think long term

'The really great businesspeople, they don't think in quarters. They think in decades.'

Warren Buffett

Thank yous

To my wife, Sarah – Your belief in me is what drove me to finish this book, especially when I doubted myself. Thank you.

To my kids, Evelyn, Josephine & Roscoe – 'Do hard things'.

To Raine, the team at Quantum, and all the test readers – Your input made this book infinitely better. Thank you.

No AI was used in the production of this book. I painstakingly wrote each word in a three-year process.

First published in 2025 by Cian Brennan

© Cian Brennan 2025

The moral rights of the author have been asserted

All rights reserved. Except as permitted under the Australian *Copyright Act 1968* (for example, a fair dealing for the purposes of study, research, criticism or review), no part of this book may be reproduced, stored in a retrieval system, communicated or transmitted in any form or by any means without prior written permission. No part of this book may be used or reproduced in any manner for the purpose of training artificial intelligence technologies or systems.

All inquiries should be made to the author.

For permission requests, email the publisher at support@quantumcontracts.com

A catalogue entry for this book is available from the
National Library of Australia.

ISBN: 978-1-923225-69-5

Printed in Australia by Pegasus

Book production and text design by Publish Central

Cover design by Pipeline Design

The paper this book is printed on is certified as environmentally friendly.

Disclaimer
The material in this publication is of the nature of general comment only, and does not represent professional advice. It is not intended to provide specific guidance for particular circumstances and it should not be relied on as the basis for any decision to take action or not take action on any matter which it covers. Readers should obtain professional advice where appropriate, before making any such decision. To the maximum extent permitted by law, the author and publisher disclaim all responsibility and liability to any person, arising directly or indirectly from any person taking or not taking action based on the information in this publication.

Contents

Start here 1

    Who is this book for? 3

    Why does this matter? 4

    What will this book do for you? 6

    How I got here 7

    This book is a tool 18

    Simplicity 20

    Important definitions used in the book 21

Chapter 1: How the game is stacked against you 25

    Chapter 1 summary 26

    Highlights 26

    A rigged game 27

    The pricing game 29

    Cashflow is oxygen for subcontractors 32

    Understanding the players in the game 34

    How main contractors maximise profit 35

    Don't be a commodity 38

    Hostile contracts 39

Chapter 2: Breaking free from the bidding trap 43

Chapter 2 summary 44

Highlights.. 44

How to win without competing on price 45

A new, improved business model 47

The money side of construction 47

The old process 51

The Quantum Contract System 54

Chapter 3: The psychology of pricing 59

Chapter 3 summary 60

Highlights.. 60

Why premium pricing works..61

How buyers make their decisions.. 67

Using marketing to promote your premium service........................ 68

Improving your proposals and bid submissions............................... 69

Building strong, respectful, long-term relationships........................71

Submitting an alternative bid... 73

Contents

Chapter 4: The silent risk 75

    Chapter 4 summary 76

    Highlights 76

    How avoiding negotiation can cost you more than you think 77

    Understanding how the other side views you 79

    How to negotiate successfully 81

    The semi-submissive approach 84

    Structuring your negotiation document 86

    What to negotiate: the three key categories 87

Chapter 5: Setting up long-term wins 91

    Chapter 5 summary 92

    Highlights 92

    Turn the kickoff meeting into the start of your new sales strategy 93

    Controlling the kickoff meeting 95

    Handling buyer's remorse 101

    Setting the agenda 104

Chapter 6: The secret weapon 109

    Chapter 6 summary 110

    Highlights 110

    Using changes and delays to your advantage 111

    Mastering the contract 113

How to do it the right way 120

Test the waters early 121

Staying on top of changes and delays 125

Chapter 7: How to avoid disputes 127

Chapter 7 summary 128

Highlights 128

How disputes drain cashflow, reputations, and relationships 129

The de-escalation conversation 131

Staying out of court 134

The GROW Model 136

Chapter 8: From bidding wars to trusted partnerships 141

Chapter 8 summary 142

Highlights 142

How to stop chasing projects and start building relationships that last 143

Check-ins one and two 148

Check-in three: the upsell 150

Check-in four: finalising the framework agreement 156

Contents

Chapter 9: The road map 159

Chapter 9 summary 160

Phase 1: secure upfront payments on new projects 162

Phase 2: negotiate better contract terms 163

Phase 3: implement a system for changes and delays 164

Phase 4: the kickoff meeting – your secret weapon 165

Phase 5: master the check-ins and the upsell 166

Phase 6: build your premium brand 167

Phase 7: master dispute avoidance 167

Phase 8: transition to framework agreements and cultivate relationships 168

Implementing this roadmap 170

What's next? 171

Where are you now? 172

Final thoughts 174

Bonus chapter: Commercial principles 175

Contract sections for ~~dummies~~ legends 176

'It is not the strongest of the species that survive, nor the most intelligent, but the one most responsive to change.'

Charles Darwin

This isn't a 'how to do construction' book. It's not a manual on delivering your services or perfecting your craft on-site.

Construction has countless disciplines, each with its own complexities and expertise. It would be foolish of me to pretend I know more about what you do than you.

This book is about the money-making side of construction. In our industry, you can deliver top-quality work but still find yourself broke, stressed, and struggling to survive.

From the start, though, let's be clear:

The foundation of any successful construction business is the quality of your work.

That's non-negotiable. Without this, nothing else matters.

So while I won't be focusing on it, it's important to understand that everything we cover in this book relies on you delivering excellent results.

As Naval Ravikant, a renowned venture capitalist who invested early in Twitter (X) and Uber, once tweeted:

> If you're good, you don't need to worry about selling. You only sell if you can't create a product (or service) that markets itself. You only market if your product (or service) isn't good enough to sell itself.

Your ability to deliver great work is your most powerful tool. It's the foundation of everything in your business.

But once you've mastered your craft, the next challenge is building and maintaining a profitable and sustainable business around it.

This book is about the 'money' side of construction – because we know that great work alone isn't enough to guarantee fair payment, steady cashflow, or protection from risks that could threaten your company.

Who is this book for?

You've already solved the first big challenge in business: you have a service or product that people want and are willing to pay for.

But now you've hit a wall.

You're probably working on projects big enough that you no longer set the terms. You're taking work from larger companies, playing by their rules, and feeling like you're stuck trying to make it all work.

Maybe you feel like you're constantly chasing jobs, bidding low to stay competitive.

Your margins are razor-thin.

Cashflow is so tight that paying your team at the end of the month feels like a juggling act.

You know one wrong move – a missed payment, a slow client, or a dispute – could put you under or set you back five years.

Does any of this sound familiar?

Even if you're not at this point, you might feel it coming.

If you own or run a subcontracting construction company, this book is for you.

If you're in a leadership role, aspiring to be in one, or working in the 'money' side of your business, this book is for you.

The strategies in this book are going to help you navigate these waters, prepare you for those bigger opportunities, and show you how to avoid the mistakes that sink so many construction businesses.

Why does this matter?

Let me break down why this matters.

Right now, your biggest challenges likely revolve around four things:

- How to increase your margins so you can stop stressing about profits.
- How to improve your cashflow so you're not always waiting to get paid.
- How to avoid landmines in contracts and projects that could derail everything.
- How to do all of this while working less and building a business that's stable, even in downturns, without relying on bidding lower just to win work or using your extra time to maintain or grow the business.

Here's the typical story of a construction company owner.

You were a highly skilled tradesperson with strong commercial instincts. You watched the company you worked for and thought, *I could do this better*. So, you did.

You started your own business, worked hard, and built a reputation for quality. The jobs started coming in, and your business grew.

But then you hit a point where it wasn't just about you anymore. The work piled up. You're working non-stop, wearing every hat – operations, sales, managing the team – and you're starting to burn out.

The company's growth has stalled. Quality issues start creeping in. Margins are shrinking. Cashflow is tighter than ever. Maybe you're dealing with disputes more than you'd like. The stress is mounting.

This is where most companies either figure it out, or fail. The majority never make it past this point. The owner becomes trapped in a business they built, unable to scale and barely able to survive.

What will this book do for you?

I know it can feel like you're running in place, working harder and harder but not seeing the results you deserve.

Here's what this book will do:

- Identify the problems that are eating into your margins, crushing your cashflow, and putting your business at risk.
- Show you the levers you can pull to regain control.
- Provide step-by-step strategies you can implement immediately to start seeing results.

By the end of this book, you won't just have ideas. You'll have a *roadmap*.

You'll know exactly what to do to transform your business from a high-stress, low-margin operation to a stable, profitable company that works for you – not the other way around.

This book isn't just theory – it's real-world, battle-tested strategies learned from the results of over 300 construction companies.

The next question you might have is: 'Why should I pay attention to you?' Many people preach from textbooks and theories, but not from real life.

Fair question …

How I got here

Construction runs in my blood. My family has been involved in the industry since 1947, starting with my grandfather's company, Brennan Construction, based in Galway, Ireland. Growing up, I saw firsthand the hard work and grit that went into building projects – but I also witnessed the challenges and the darker side of the business.

James Brennan (Contractors) Ltd.

Building and Civil Engineering Contractors

Established 1947

Spanish Parade
Galway

Tel. (091) 62625; 7812

James Brennan, P.C.
Chairman

At 12 years old, I started working on construction sites during my school holidays, eager to make some money. I swept floors, moved materials, and became the 'go-for' for any tradesperson who needed something done, even if it meant buying cigarettes from the shop. A year in, I was driving heavy machinery around the sites, which would probably get most construction projects shut down nowadays. I loved the hard work and feeling of being exhausted when I got home.

However, construction wasn't just about hard work; it was about the struggles and risks involved. My grandfather's company faced challenges. A major dispute eventually caused the company to go out of business, leaving a cloud of financial uncertainty and strain that lingered over my family.

I didn't fully understand what had happened back then, but I could see the impact it had on everyone around me. The loss affected more than just the company; it shook our family. Once I understood this later, I was determined to learn why this had happened and how I could prevent similar situations for other families.

My dream was to start my own company in the industry, but I followed my father's advice to avoid the contracting side of construction and instead work for the owners. I went into higher education, earning degrees in construction economics and management and a master's in engineering management.

Over the years, I worked for or consulted with some of the biggest names in the industry, including 13 of the top 30 construction companies worldwide. I climbed the corporate ladder, becoming a director in a well-known consultancy and an expert in contract strategy, and developed cost-saving measures that made major projects more profitable. But while my career was advancing, I couldn't shake the feeling I was playing for the wrong team.

When I started my career, I wanted what most people want: to be successful in my job, a steady income, and the ability to provide for my family. But when I was sent a newspaper clipping from the day my grandfather died that said, 'Death of man who helped build Galway', I realised I had forgotten my dream of following in my grandfather's footsteps to build something meaningful that could outlast me and change the industry for the better.

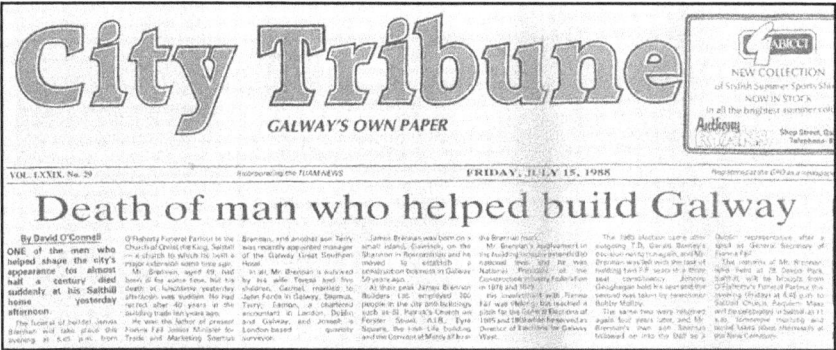

As time went on, it wasn't enough to succeed on a personal level. I wanted to build a business that changed the construction industry for the better. I wanted to help contractors – the ones who did the actual work.

Working for large construction companies gave me a front-row seat to the exploitation of contractors (the definitions of these terms are at the end of this chapter). These companies routinely shifted risks onto smaller contractors to protect their own margins.

When disputes arose, the contractors were often the ones left holding the bag. I saw family-owned businesses crumble because they weren't paid for completed work, couldn't navigate complex contractual disputes, or had agreed to contracts filled with unfair terms.

It was a brutal reality, and it was becoming increasingly difficult for me to ignore. The contractors were the backbone of the industry, yet they were often treated as expendable.

It wasn't just one or two companies that fell into this trap. I watched it happen repeatedly: small businesses with hardworking owners who had poured everything into their companies, only to watch them collapse under the weight of bad contracts or unpaid invoices.

Many contractors operated on razor-thin margins, and any unexpected delays or disputes could easily push them into insolvency. The industry seemed designed to crush these companies, and I was on the wrong side of that system.

As my career progressed, I found myself wrestling with a growing sense of disillusionment. I had built a life that was successful on paper, but I wasn't happy.

I was contributing to the very system that had devastated my family years ago. I was working with companies whose practices didn't align with the values I had been raised with: hard work, fairness, and treating people with respect.

The projects I worked on often required me to be away from my family for extended periods. I spent months at a time in places like the Pilbara in Western Australia, Saudi Arabia, Qatar, and the United Arab Emirates, chasing lucrative contracts but missing out on important family moments.

I had a baby girl at home, and each time I left for a project, I felt the weight of what I was sacrificing. The money was good, but it came at a steep personal cost.

I was physically present in these distant places, but emotionally, I felt lost. I wasn't proud of what I was doing, and I wasn't proud of who I was becoming.

My breaking point came during one of the riskiest decisions of my career. I took on a high-stakes role in Iraq, a country still reeling from conflict, where danger was a constant companion.

The job was on a massive oil and gas project that required awarding contracts to hundreds of contractors, covering everything from civil works to steel fabrication to material and equipment supply. It wasn't just another project; it was a test of endurance and nerve.

I knew the risks, but I thought that if I could earn the money to start and build a business, it would be worth it. I would also be able to spend time figuring out what that business would be.

Being in Iraq was unlike any other experience. I wore a bulletproof vest to work and navigated sites scarred by war, where every step could reveal another reminder of the conflict.

The work itself was gruelling, and the atmosphere was tense. Every day felt like a race against time and a battle against chaos.

There were moments when the sound of distant explosions would disrupt the monotony of construction noise, making me acutely aware of how far I was from the safety of home.

Was that a construction noise? Was that something else? How far away was it?

On top of the personal strain, I saw contractors facing the same harsh reality. Three or four companies went out of business while I was there. They couldn't pay their workers, lost money, and were crushed by the larger construction companies.

Watching these businesses, full of hope and hard work, collapse so quickly was painful. It reinforced my feeling that something had to change – for them and for me.

One evening, I was having a conversation with a mentor (someone I discuss later in this book), and found myself curious about the large contract teams we had. Most of the time they dwarfed the subcontractors 10 to 1.

I asked him: 'Why do we need so many people dedicated to contracts?'

It seemed excessive – a massive overhead – and I wondered why these companies would invest so heavily in something that didn't immediately look profitable.

He looked at me and said plainly: 'On every project, 15% of the profit is up for grabs.'

He went on to explain that in the 2000s the big management consultancies came in and advised main contractors that a contracts system is where the profitability is in construction projects.

When they say 'contract system', they don't just mean the contracts themselves.

I'm talking about a comprehensive system – one that includes managing risk, building long-term client relationships, cashflow management, quicker payments, and dispute procedures.

It's kinda like having an autopilot that just takes care of money flow and risk on a project.

That 15% figure stopped me in my tracks. If this system impacts profits that significantly, then the resources make sense.

I dug into the research, and sure enough, he was right. Main contractors were investing heavily in contract systems because they understood how much was at stake.

Here is some of that data:

- A **McKinsey & Company** report shows that construction companies can lose **5% to 10%** of project value due to inefficiencies like change orders and poor contract management.[1]

- The **Construction Industry Institute** (CII) found that companies with solid contract administration practices see up to a **15%** improvement in project profitability. This comes from faster payment processing, compensation for valid project changes, and fewer disputes.[2]

- According to the **American Subcontractors Association** (ASA), nearly 40% of subcontractors face delayed payments, which erode profits by **5% to 15%**.[3]

---

1   McKinsey & Company, 'Reinventing Construction: A Route to Higher Productivity', February 2017.
2   Construction Industry Institute, 'Benchmarking & Metrics Summary Report', January 2014.
3   American Subcontractors Association, 'The ASA Subcontractor's Negotiating Tips'.

Then I had an epiphany: subcontractors were losing out on this same profit opportunity every time they took on a project, simply because they didn't have a comparable contract system in place.

Subcontractors need this same kind of system. In today's construction world, it's become essential. Without it, subcontractors are at a constant disadvantage, essentially giving up 15% on every project on day one.

I knew I had all the insider tools and knowledge to help subcontractors navigate the complex contract systems that larger companies used to keep subcontractors at a disadvantage.

So I quit and returned to Australia with no job and only an idea for a business.

But there was another problem. For years, I watched subcontractors struggle – not just due to a lack of expertise but because they simply didn't have the resources to afford the level of skill and support needed to compete effectively.

The owners of these subcontracting companies had to do this work themselves or outsource it to a person on their team as a 'side hustle' to their day-to-day job.

Hiring people is very expensive, and engaging consultants on day rates even moreso.

I created a solution.

I had seen other businesses in different industries use a fractional service model, so I developed a similar system to give subcontractors access to a contract system without needing a full-time team.

Subcontractors were able to get top-tier advice, all the paperwork done, and strategic support through a flexible monthly retainer they could turn on or off as needed.

Now they could compete directly with the bigger companies and get that extra profit. Toe to toe.

Building this company (Quantum Contracts) and system wasn't without its struggles, but the challenges weren't about growing the company itself – they were about changing a mindset that was deeply embedded in the industry.

The real battle was convincing subcontractors that they didn't have to accept contracts as they were given.

Many had grown used to the idea that contracts were non-negotiable and that pushing back would only jeopardise their relationships with larger contractors.

There was a long-standing belief that accepting whatever terms were offered was simply part of the business. My challenge was to shift that perspective.

There were skeptics who thought we were wasting our time and that subcontractors would always be considered disposable. But I had seen the industry from the inside; I knew how much room there was for improvement, and I was convinced that change was possible.

As word spread about my system, subcontractors began to push back more frequently, refusing to accept unfavourable terms and getting smarter with how they operated their contracts.

This didn't go unnoticed.

At one point, I received a call from a company I had previously worked with – a major player in the industry. They weren't happy. They asked me to stop what I was doing, to shut down the business, and to abandon the work we were doing for subcontractors.

They warned that if I didn't comply, there would be consequences. They didn't elaborate on what those consequences would be, but the message was clear: they wanted us to back down.

I wasn't about to give up on a mission that had become so personal. I knew I was on the right path, and I wasn't going to let vague threats derail what we had started. The call only reinforced my resolve to keep pushing forward.

It wasn't just about business anymore; it was about standing up to a system that had been rigged against smaller companies for far too long.

Quantum Contracts quickly became a leader in the construction industry, expanding across the US, Australia, Canada, New Zealand, and the UK. By 2023, we had reviewed and managed over 7000 contracts worth more than $30 billion.

As far as I am aware, at the time of writing there is no other company offering what we do to subcontractors using such a model. I am sure that will change.

Our efforts garnered industry recognition, including two Telstra Best of Business Awards; one for outstanding growth and another for innovation. I was also honoured to be listed among the *Business News* Top 40 Entrepreneurs Under 40. Sadly, I am no longer eligible for that award.

Looking back, I see how I've changed in ways I never expected. Initially, my drive was to follow in my grandfather's footsteps and build something that would honour his legacy.

I wanted to be part of the industry he loved, but I imagined doing it from within the system, working with the largest players.

Over time, though, I realised that honouring his legacy wasn't about climbing corporate ranks or increasing margins for big firms. It was about supporting the people who actually made construction happen – the subcontractors who brought projects to life and carried the real weight of this industry.

I came to understand that my place was on their side, standing up for the trades, not the corporations.

In making this shift, I didn't just change my career path; I became a different person.

I let go of the need to play by the rules set by big industry players and embraced values that felt true to me: integrity, fairness, and loyalty to those who keep construction alive.

It was no longer just about succeeding; it was about succeeding the right way. I found a sense of purpose that didn't conflict with who I was or the values I'd been raised with, and for the first time, I felt like I was building a legacy I could be proud of.

Now, I'm not going to pretend I have all the answers. In fact, I've made my fair share of mistakes along the way – some big, some small.

I've made poor decisions, hurt people unintentionally, and at times even acted with good intentions that led to bad outcomes.

I'm human, battle demons every day, and have many shortcomings. But despite all that, I've managed to get really good at one thing: helping contractors protect their businesses and thrive in an industry designed to work against them. And that's what I'm here to share with you.

So, while I may not be perfect, I know this: the strategies in this book aren't just ideas – they're battle-tested tools that can help you avoid the same pitfalls I've seen take down so many others.

Let's dive in, and I'll show you how.

> **YOU'RE ALREADY IN THE TOP 30%**
>
> Did you know that 70% of people buy books but never read them, and another 20% only make it through the first few chapters?
>
> If you're reading this now, congratulations – you're already in the top 30%.
>
> **Promise:** The further you go, the better the insights get. Keep reading, and you'll see for yourself.

This book is a tool

This isn't just a book to read once and set aside. It's a tool – one you'll want to come back to again and again.

The ideas and strategies inside are meant to be put into action, not just passively absorbed. Business success requires ongoing effort and the right resources, and this book is one of those key resources.

Whether you're facing new challenges or refining your approach, you'll find yourself returning to these pages for guidance and clarity.

Remember, the real value lies in applying what you learn – so treat this book as a living resource to support your progress.

> **MORE TOOLS**
>
> Research has shown that engaging with material in multiple formats – such as reading, listening, and watching – significantly enhances comprehension and retention.
>
> In fact, a study conducted by the University of California found that when you consume information through written, audio, and visual formats simultaneously, you can improve learning efficiency **by up to 40%**.
>
> For that reason, I have also created this book in audiobook format. If you're like me and struggle to focus on one thing, or read a few pages and forget what you've just read instantly, listening to the book at the same time as reading it significantly increases retention and reading speed.
>
> Search for *The Subcontractor's Edge* on Audible to get the audiobook or head on over to quantumcontractsolutions.com/thesubedgeaudio to find it directly.

Simplicity

As you go through this book, you may notice something. It presents information using pictures (done by me!) and simple words.

Consultants are the reason for this, and specifically my disdain for them (even though I was one).

I have had many consultants come into my businesses over time and with very little success. They talk in jargon, making simple things complex. When you ask basic questions, they struggle to answer.

The reason is, they don't actually know the answer.

Professor Richard Feynman was famous for his work on quantum electrodynamics. He said:

> If you cannot explain something in simple terms, you don't understand it.

For me the success of this book is about you being able to implement the strategies. If I can't explain it simply, how are you going to take the information and put it in place?

My aim in writing this book is simplicity, so that it can be easily implemented. That's my reason for the simple words and pictures.

Important definitions used in the book

We really don't make it easy for ourselves in the construction industry, do we? We call the same thing different names in different countries, and oftentimes even within that country we call them different things again.

To simplify the issue, here is a list of the terms I will use throughout the book:

- **Owner:** This is the company that is the ultimate owner of the asset being constructed. For example: the apartment block (developer); the bridge (the government); the oil and gas plant (oil company); or the factory (public company).

- **Main contractor:** This is the construction company that wins the whole project from the owner and then subcontracts out the work.

  This contractor is commonly referred to as a general contractor in the US, a tier 1 contractor in the literature, and the main contractor in most other countries. I've gone with 'main contractor' as it will resonate with more people. Sorry US!

- **Subcontractors:** These are my people, and who this book is for. These are the companies that win work typically from the main contractor but sometimes (if they are savvy) directly from the owner.

  They are commonly referred to as contactors (confusing, right?), subcontractors, suppliers (a subcontractor that only supplies but doesn't install), and tier 2 or 3 contractors in the literature. 'Subcontractors' makes the most sense and we will use this.

- **Framework agreement:** A framework agreement is a long-term agreement between two parties. It agrees upfront the general terms and conditions and has a mechanism to easily issue contracts called 'call offs' or 'purchase/service orders'.

  A framework is typically agreed when one company trusts and wants to create a longer-term relationship with a subcontractor. The purpose is to easily and quickly engage the subcontractor to do work without having to go through the contract negotiation phase.

  I'm speculating here of course but I think lawyers make things more complicated just to confuse the rest of us – look at this bloody list of different names for the same thing that I've come across in my career:

  - ☐ master services agreement
  - ☐ master agreement
  - ☐ standing offer agreement
  - ☐ call-off agreement
  - ☐ master supply agreement
  - ☐ term agreement
  - ☐ panel contract
  - ☐ outline agreement
  - ☐ blanket purchase agreement
  - ☐ umbrella agreement.

  Anyway, I've gone with 'framework agreement'.

- **Bidding:** When a subcontractor gives a proposal to do work. You may be asked to do so as part of a competitive tender or sole-sourced project.

    This can also be called quoting, submitting a proposal, or a response. For the purpose of the book I am going to use 'bidding'.

- **Pre-award:** All activities before you sign the contract.
- **Post-award:** All activities after you sign the contract.
- **Client:** When I use the term 'client' in this book, I am referring to the company who has awarded the contract to you.
- **Commercial:** Depending on the country, this can mean different things. When used in the book, I am referring to anything related to dollars and cents.
- **Project director:** The person leading the project for the main contractor. The project director manages the project team and is the main contact for the owner.

    Other names for this role include project lead and construction director.

- **Clause:** In a contract there are numbered paragraphs specific to a particular topic. These are called clauses or sections. I will refer to them as 'clauses'.
- **Upsell:** Many subcontractors shy away from sales, so I use a term that emphasises that you are indeed selling your services. In the book the 'upsell' refers to selling your client on a long-term relationship.

In the next chapter, we'll explore the challenges subcontractors face in the construction industry. You'll learn how the game is rigged against you and how to shift from low bids to strategies that improve cashflow, protect margins, and grow your business on autopilot.

Chapter 1

How the game is stacked against you

Chapter 1 summary

In this chapter, you'll uncover the tough realities of the construction industry and the challenges faced by subcontractors.

It reveals how the system is often stacked against you, with subcontractors bearing most of the risk while fighting to maintain cashflow and profitability.

You'll learn how to move away from low bidding and volume-driven strategies to adopt premium pricing that sets you apart in a competitive market.

Highlights

- Why the construction industry feels like a rigged game for subcontractors.
- How to avoid the low-price trap when bidding.
- Why cashflow is more critical than profit.
- How to position your business for premium pricing.
- The importance of understanding the motivations of owners and main contractors.
- How to avoid being treated as a commodity in the bidding process.

> 'The difficulty lies not so much in developing new ideas as in escaping from old ones.'

John Maynard Keynes

A rigged game

The US Bureau of Labor Statistics reports that 26% of all business failures happen in construction, making it the highest-failure industry. In fact, 67% of construction companies fail within 10 years, most within the first five.

Only 3.3 out of 10 construction companies survive. These are often smaller companies, usually working as subcontracted providers.

You're playing a rigged game that's stacked against you. If this chapter helps you understand the game, the rest of the book will show you how to avoid the mistakes that lead to failure. With only 3 out of 10 construction companies making it, you'll get valuable lessons here – without the scars.

Watching yet another company fold up their tent

I stood in the side office, watching through a cracked window as another family-owned construction company packed up their gear and walked off the site. I knew it was the last time I'd see them here.

Their team – faces etched with frustration and resignation – was leaving in silence, knowing they were walking away from a project that had drained them dry. Financially, they were done, and deep down, I think we all saw it coming.

The Subcontractor's Edge

It wasn't the first time I'd witnessed this. In the last six months, they were the fourth company to walk off the site. And the truth is, from the very beginning it was clear the odds were against them.

I was on the other side of the table. While I wasn't trying to be the bad guy, my team and I were under immense pressure from management to cut costs.

We were part of a bigger system where budgets ruled all decisions – getting subcontractors to come in lower was part of the process.

During the bidding phase, the privately run business had submitted one of the lowest bids, but we were working within tight constraints and saw an opportunity to push them just a little further.

We weren't trying to be ruthless; we were simply doing what was expected of us in a project that was already over budget.

The negotiation began respectfully. They had already come in at a price that left little room for margins, but we still had to ask for more. We offered promises of future work and reassurances to help justify our ask.

I could see their hesitation, and it didn't feel right, but the pressure to reduce costs was relentless. Eventually, they agreed, hoping it would all balance out once they were on-site.

But it didn't.

The project moved forward as they always do – delays hit, unexpected costs cropped up.

And as we feared, the company's slim margins couldn't absorb the impact. By the time it became clear they were in over their heads, it was too late to turn back.

They were stuck in a contract that offered no way out.

And now, as I stood watching them pack up and leave, I couldn't shake the feeling that our system had pushed them over the edge. I told myself I was just doing my job, playing my part in a larger process, but the weight of it lingered.

I wished there had been another way.

There was. I just didn't know it yet.

The pricing game

There are different pricing and business models, which I will discuss later in this chapter. For now, it's important to understand the difference between a *premium pricing model* and a *volume pricing model*.

Right now, you're likely bidding low to win jobs. That's the **volume game**. But you can't play a premium game with volume prices.

Competitive tenders almost always award work to the lowest-priced technically qualified companies. If all subcontractors offer the same service, the job will go to the one with the lowest profit margin.

Construction companies are not built to play the volume game. Construction is a **premium game**.

The volume game is when your entire company is optimised for low prices. Think of Walmart in the US, Tesco in the UK, or Woolworths in Australia and New Zealand. These companies make a small margin but earn through massive volume.

However, in construction you won't have the volume needed to operate on low margins. You'd need an extremely large volume for those low margins to be sustainable.

There are four different types of pricing games you can play:

1. **Low cost, high volume:** These companies make money by having smaller margins but much higher volumes. Examples include Walmart, Tesco, Woolworths, Hyundai and Kia.

2. **No man's land:** These companies don't price high for larger margins, nor are they optimised for low-cost, high-volume models. This is where most construction companies find themselves.

3. **Premium products:** Companies that charge higher margins because their products are premium. BMW and Mercedes are great examples. These cars are successful because they are well-made and offer a premium experience compared to a Hyundai or a Kia.

4. **Luxury goods:** These products are expensive, and the higher the price, the more desirable they become. Rolls Royce and Louis Vuitton are prime examples. In this space, raising prices increases demand.

Have you ever encountered a client who expected premium service, high-quality results, and top-tier gear – but still wanted you to come in at the lowest price?

It's frustrating, but it happens often. Any business's goal is to make a profit, and the best way to do that is to play the right game. In construction, the right game is premium pricing.

Subcontractor profit margins are notoriously low. In the US, profit margins for subcontractors fall between 6% and 9%. In the UK, it's even lower at 2% to 3%, and in Australia, margins range from 6% to 8%. With such slim margins, it's impossible to deliver the premium results your clients expect.

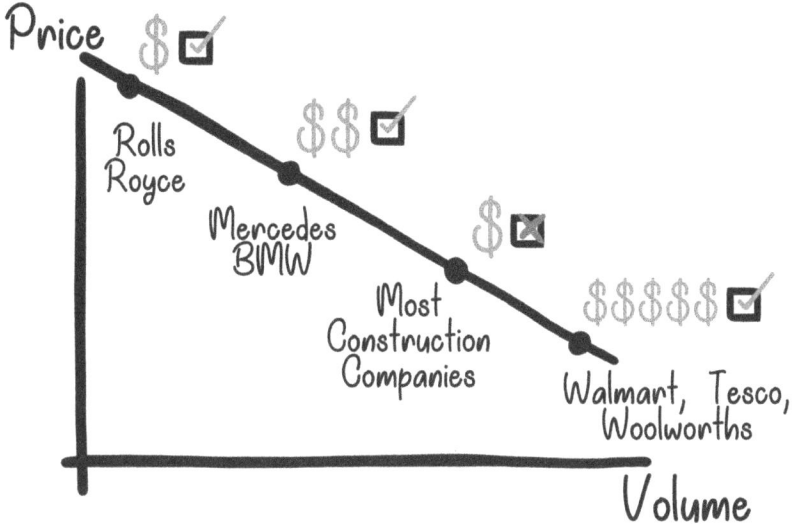

The current construction bidding system doesn't work for subcontractors or suppliers unless they are optimised for low cost at every stage of the value chain. Even then, they need enough volume to make the small-margin jobs profitable.

You might be wondering, *How can I win a tender if I raise my prices? I'll never win a bid.* In this book, you'll learn a strategy to move away from competitive tendering.

There will always be competition, but I'll show you how to recover the profit you sacrifice at the bidding stage during the post-award phase.

Here's a quick exercise.

Look at the margin of your last five projects:

- Where did you expect your margin to be at the start?
- Where did it end up at the completion of the project?

Does this margin allow you to invest in premium people, equipment, and materials?

You want to build a reputation for quality, but this exercise may reveal that you're playing a losing game. Understanding these numbers is what will keep you from going broke. This is a great baseline to start from, and by the end of this book, you'll have the tools to change the game.

Cashflow is oxygen for subcontractors

After 20 years working on the client side with subcontractors, I've seen many subcontractors and suppliers go out of business. Their leaders often say they couldn't pay their workers and had to walk off the job. At Quantum, many clients tell us they are on the brink of going under. Others say they feel strangled by cashflow issues.

When construction companies fail, it doesn't happen suddenly. It's a slow process, like being choked by a lack of cashflow. The money gets tighter and tighter until the company can't breathe anymore. Cashflow is the most important metric in construction. If cash is king, cashflow is the oxygen the king needs to breathe. It's everything.

Many construction companies, subcontractors, and suppliers operate with a poor business model. Let's look at a few common models, from worst to best:

- **Deferred payment model:** 'I'll work for free for 30, 60, or 90 days, and then you'll pay me.' This is how most people in construction operate.

- **Prepaid payment model:** 'Pay me first, and then I'll do the work.' This is how most online businesses work nowadays – you pay upfront, and they provide the service after.

- **Insurance payment model:** 'Pay me upfront, and I may never need to do the work.' Think of insurance companies. You pay upfront and hope you never need their services.

If you're reading this, your business probably relies on the first model. If you can shift your business model, you can change your cashflow.

More cashflow means less stress. You can pay your people on time, deliver better projects, lower your bank financing costs, and give yourself more room to recover if something goes wrong on a project – because we all know things go wrong.

Years ago, I worked for a large oil and gas company. I once hired a supplier to build and maintain a turbine. When we went to tender, I was surprised at their business model.

It was simple: 'Give us a downpayment to start building the turbine. Pay us in milestones before we finish. Then pay us exclusively for 20 years to maintain it.'

This model is brilliant, and it's something construction companies can aim for. They always have money before they spend it, so their cashflow stays high. They get a big payment upfront and continue to earn for years. This is why companies like General Electric and Siemens are so profitable and valuable.

You might be thinking, *That's not how it works in my industry. My clients won't agree to an upfront payment.*

I had this conversation with two CEOs. One said, 'I can't ask for that. They'll never agree.'

The other said, 'We ask all the time, and we get it most of the time.'

Same type of business, same industry. If you don't ask, you won't get. The key is in *how you ask*, and that's what I'll teach you in this book.

To figure out what model you're currently using, ask yourself these three questions:

- Have you ever asked for an upfront payment?
- Have you ever received an upfront payment?
- If yes, how did it positively impact your finances and stress levels on that project?

Understanding the players in the game

Just like any game, you need to understand the other players. In this section, I'll outline the key players in the construction industry, their motivations, and how they play the game.

There are three key players in the construction game: the owner, the main contractor, and the subcontractors. The main player to watch is the company you contract with, usually the main contractor.

The **owner** is at the top. They want to build something – whether it's a block of apartments, a bridge, or an oil and gas plant. Their main motivation is getting the project completed so they can make money or use the asset. Their goal is the final product, whether it's for profit or operational use.

Next is the **main contractor**. These companies win the project and subcontract most of the work to others. Their top goal is to maximise profit, and they do this through a few strategies, which we'll explore below.

Subcontractors and suppliers are the last group. They are the ones doing the hands-on work to build the project. Their goal is to make a profit, often as family-owned or private businesses looking to leave a legacy. They either want to pass the business down to loved ones or eventually sell it to a larger contractor.

How main contractors maximise profit

The main contractor's top-level goal is to maximise profit. To do this, they focus on getting the most out of every project by managing their costs and risks.

They are essentially intermediaries, winning work from the owner, securing financing from a bank, and subcontracting the actual construction work to companies like yours.

Their profit comes from the difference between what the owner pays them, what they pay the bank, and what they pay subcontractors.

Main contractors have two core levers they use to increase their profit:

- **Financing costs:** Main contractors often secure a loan to fund the project. The cost of this financing is usually fixed, so they know how much interest and repayments they'll need to make.

    As long as the project doesn't go over budget, they know exactly how much they'll owe and how much they'll get paid by the owner.

- **Payments to subcontractors:** This is the biggest lever main contractors can adjust during the project to increase their profit. They manipulate this in two ways:

  - **Shifting risk:** Main contractors often push risk down the chain onto subcontractors.

    They write contracts that pass as much risk as possible to you, including delays, mistakes, or unforeseen circumstances. When something goes wrong, they make it your responsibility, saving them money and protecting their profit.

  - **Cost-cutting:** Main contractors aim to pay you as little as possible.

    Even after you've won the bid, they will fight you on every additional cost or change order to minimise their payouts. If the contract doesn't obligate them to pay, they won't, and they will rely on strict interpretations of the contract to avoid extra costs.

A lot of these companies have what's called a 'closeout team'. I was involved in numerous closeout teams.

This is when a team comes in at the end of the project with the sole focus of cutting costs. A closeout team will come in and say things like:

- 'I don't care about the relationship you have with this guy.'
- 'I can't rely on what has been verbally discussed or any previous arrangements.'
- 'We have to go by the book, and the contract says that you're not entitled to be paid for this change and so I'm not paying for it.'

Their job is to save the company money by denying payments they believe aren't contractually owed but are more often than not ethically owed.

It's important to understand this dynamic because, as a subcontractor, you are often the only option for the main contractor to increase their profits. And this puts them in direct conflict with you.

There's a game being played, and if you don't understand how the game works or who the players are, you're going to lose.

Many in the construction industry talk about relationships and say most people in the business are good, honest workers. While that's true, there are also plenty who would step over you for a dollar.

Not everyone will play by your rules or share your moral standards. They have their own goals, and just like you, they want to win.

When push comes to shove, profit and company pressures will almost always outweigh personal goodwill. Even good people are forced to comply with their company's demands.

Have you or any of your friends in construction ever been screwed over by someone you trusted on a handshake deal?

If it hasn't happened yet, it's only a matter of time. There was a time when verbal agreements carried weight in this industry, and a handshake was enough to seal a deal. Relationships used to mean everything. But those days are fading.

Now, handshakes and verbal commitments will not protect your business as they once did. Many have learned this the hard way.

Don't be a commodity

In the construction industry, subcontractors and suppliers are often seen as commodities. There are many other companies that seem to do the same work as you. From the client's perspective, they think you all provide the same service.

But in construction, you don't want to be treated like a commodity. Think about how people buy the commodity of a fridge – they search online to decide on the fridge they want, then search all the online stores for the cheapest price. Then they buy. The company providing the fridge at the lowest price (think margin) wins.

If clients see you as a commodity, it means they think you're interchangeable with others, and that's a problem.

When you're seen as a commodity, main contractors don't care if you go out of business. For example, if you're a civil company and there are five others in the area, they'll consider all five and pick the cheapest one.

The lowest price model only works if you're playing the volume game, but in construction, volume rarely works for subcontractors.

In the back of a client's mind, they're always thinking, *I can replace this person with someone cheaper if things don't work out*. They are thinking of you as a commodity.

The key is to find a way to stand out, to show you're different from other companies.

I've seen many cases where the main contractor pressured a subcontractor, saying something like: 'If you don't accept non-payment, stop complaining, or if you try to submit a delay claim or change order, we'll kick you off the site and replace you.'

They just want someone to do the job – hopefully at a cheaper price. Many construction companies think, *We're different. We're faster, cheaper, and higher quality.*

But is that difference clear in your bids? After reviewing thousands of bids, I can tell you: most companies say the same things on the front of their proposals.

Main contractors try to box you in as a commodity. They want you to fit their lowest-priced qualified model. To break free from this, you must show that your approach is different from the start.

Think back – have you ever been threatened with replacement because you didn't accept a condition on-site, like a change order, delay, or non-payment? If it hasn't happened yet, it probably will soon.

Hostile contracts

Hostile contracts always get pushed down to the lowest level in the construction hierarchy. Subcontractors and suppliers often end up with the most aggressive contracts in the industry, despite having the least resources to enforce or negotiate them.

Let's walk through how this happens, starting from the project's inception.

First, the owner decides to build something. They choose a main contractor, often a large company with internal lawyers and contract teams.

The owner and main contractor agree on a contract that suits both sides. At this point, the main contractor needs to subcontract the actual work to companies like yours.

In the past, industry bodies created standard contracts with reasonable terms for subcontractors and suppliers. Those were the good old days, but that model is dead. Over the past five years, after reviewing over 7000 contracts, I've only seen a handful of standard agreements.

Instead, large firms now push the risk onto subcontractors by getting them to sign what are often called 'hostile contracts'. These contracts are heavily one-sided, shifting the risk down the chain.

If something goes wrong, you bear the burden. If extra costs arise, you're the one paying for it.

Essentially, the most aggressive contracts land on your shoulders, the subcontractor, and you have the least resources to handle them.

I believe this is why the construction industry has the highest bankruptcy rate of any industry.

You need to understand this: at the bottom of the chain, you get the worst contracts, with the highest risks and the least expertise to manage them. The image opposite reflects this.

Unless you know how to fight these terms, you'll be at a severe disadvantage. Based on my experience over the years, let me

How the game is stacked against you

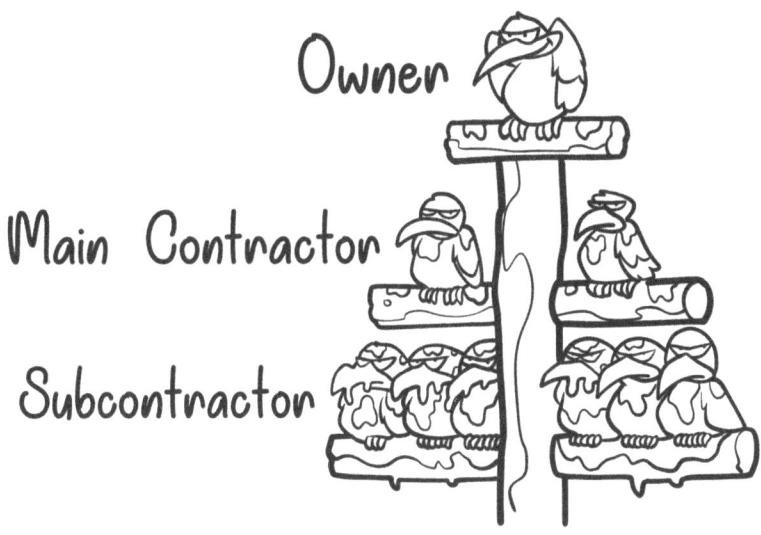

give you a few examples of just how aggressive these contracts can be.

Delays are a constant issue in the construction industry, but what happens when all the costs fall on you? What if the delays aren't your fault, but you're still stuck covering the financial impact?

I've seen contracts with time bars as short as 12 hours. A time bar means if you don't notify the main contractor about a delay or change within that timeframe, you're stuck with the cost.

Sometimes, delay clauses are written in a way that makes it nearly impossible to claim for delays, no matter the circumstances.

There are many other contract terms that can raise your costs – liquidated damages, indemnities, and excessive insurance requirements, to name a few. The bottom line is, you're often dealing with hostile contracts that shift as much risk as possible onto you.

Some might argue that standard contracts still exist, and they do. But a common, sneaky practice is to use a standard template, like the ones you're familiar with, and then amend it. It looks like the standard contract you know, but it's been changed, and if you don't read it carefully, you won't notice.

So here's my advice: commit to never signing a contract again without fully reading and negotiating it.

Even if you don't fully understand the contract now, by the end of this book, you'll know what to look for, what to negotiate, and why.

> **CHAPTER 1 ACTION ITEM: EVALUATE YOUR LAST TWO OR THREE PROJECTS FOR PROFITABILITY AND CASHFLOW.**
>
> **Step 1:** Take a look at your last two or three completed projects. Review where you expected your margin to be at the start and where it ended up.
>
> **Step 2:** Identify any discrepancies – did delays, changes, or cashflow issues impact your final margin?
>
> **Step 3:** Ask yourself: 'Could I have negotiated better terms upfront or managed the project differently to improve my margins and cashflow?'
>
> **Why:** Understanding where your margins ended up and why compared to your expectations will help you recognise how the current low-bidding system affects your profitability. This simple review process can give you insights into how to adjust your business model and move towards a premium pricing strategy.

Chapter 2
Breaking free from the bidding trap

Chapter 2 summary

In this chapter, we explore the transition from the traditional construction business model of competitive bidding to a new, sustainable model focused on building long-term client relationships and securing future projects.

Highlights

- Why moving away from competitive bidding is essential for business growth.
- How to build long-term client relationships that lead to repeat projects.
- How to manage contracts to maximise margins.
- Why choosing the right clients can make or break your future workload.

> 'It's not about having the right opportunities. It's about handling the opportunities right.'
>
> Mark Hunter

How to win without competing on price

How do you shift from what you're currently doing to a new, sustainable, and profitable model?

You start by using the old method of competitive bidding to get in the door. Then, change your approach. Focus on building long-term relationships with this new client so you won't have to bid competitively in the future.

In this chapter, I'll break down the model you're currently stuck in. I'll show you where to disrupt the process and how to move away from competitive bidding. I'll also share strategies to improve your cashflow on all your future projects.

However, there's one important thing to consider with this model: *you must choose clients who can offer you future work*. These clients should have multiple projects or be bigger main contractors who move from project to project.

If a client only has a few projects and they can't provide more work later, it's a waste of time beyond the margin on that current job.

As I mentioned in chapter 1, only 3 out of 10 construction companies survive more than 10 years. If you stick to the standard model, you'll get the standard results. Something needs to change.

You can't just raise your prices and expect everything to improve. You need a process to shift from the old way of doing business, and I'm going to outline it at a high level in this chapter.

Let me introduce Kentz Engineering. They started in a small town in Ireland, called Clonmel, and grew into markets like the Middle East, Australia, Canada, and the US. In 2014, they sold their company for $6 billion to a Canadian construction firm.

I consulted for them back in 2012. Their model was simple: they priced their projects low, knowing they could recover their margins in the post-award phase with strong contract management skills.

A key component is negotiating the correct things with regards to changes and delays within the contract, and they were experts at this. They knew this was crucial to set themselves up for success in the post-award phase.

Almost every subcontractor makes a bet that the project will go perfectly. If it doesn't, they take a hit.

Kentz turned the tables with their strategy. They bet that it wouldn't go perfectly, and when that scenario occurs they stand to make a lot of money.

They invested in a contracts team to handle their projects. They ensured all changes and delays were submitted very quickly and paid for quickly. A massive help to cashflow.

This model worked well – they bid low to win work, then made up their margin through changes and delays.

This approach also highlights the importance of building relationships. Once they established a relationship with a client, their goal was to secure more projects with that same client.

A new, improved business model

In this chapter, we're going to dive into a new, improved business model for you. We'll compare it with the old way, which involved winning projects by bidding the lowest, with slim margins.

The old model creates peaks and troughs in your business – when you're only bidding, there are times when no projects are available and business slumps. Then, suddenly, when many projects become available, you're riding the wave.

I'm going to show you a new way to manage this. I'll walk you through the timeline of events, covering negotiations, project kickoffs, and a game-changing upsell strategy.

This upsell will help you build long-term relationships and break away from the low-price model.

The money side of construction

There are many ways to improve your business. You can pull different levers to make a real difference. The model overleaf is a triangle that highlights the money-making parts of your business and how you can adjust these levers to increase profitability.

The main drivers of most construction businesses, once you have enough opportunities, are:

- **Margin:** Margin is about having enough profit to justify staying in business. It also means having sufficient profit to invest in better equipment, people, and systems. This investment improves your work for clients and strengthens your reputation. A virtuous cycle begins: as your reputation improves, more clients will come to you, and you'll be able to make more money in the future.

- **Cashflow:** Cashflow is the lifeblood of a construction company. Without healthy cashflow, companies struggle to survive. Payment terms, prepayments, and financing all impact cashflow. When cashflow is strong, it reduces stress, allows you to be more selective about the projects you take on, and gives you more flexibility in how you handle day-to-day work.

- **Risk:** If you want to sell your business in the future, hand it down to a loved one, or just grow your profit, you need to manage your risk. The construction industry is one of the riskiest industries in the world. You've got project changes, weather delays, workers, strikes, accidents, and escalation of labour rates.

Let's be real: something bad will happen over the next 5 or 10 years. I don't think anyone will argue with me about that. The question is, will your company be mortally wounded, or will it just be a small cut? You must protect your downside.

Let me walk you through this model quickly. On the outside of the triangle we have cashflow, margin, and risk. To use this model, we need be asking ourselves these questions:

- How do we increase our cashflow?
- How do we boost our margin and risk tolerance?
- How do we reduce our risk?

This model shows which levers to pull to improve your business. It identifies actions that can increase cashflow, boost margins, and lower risk.

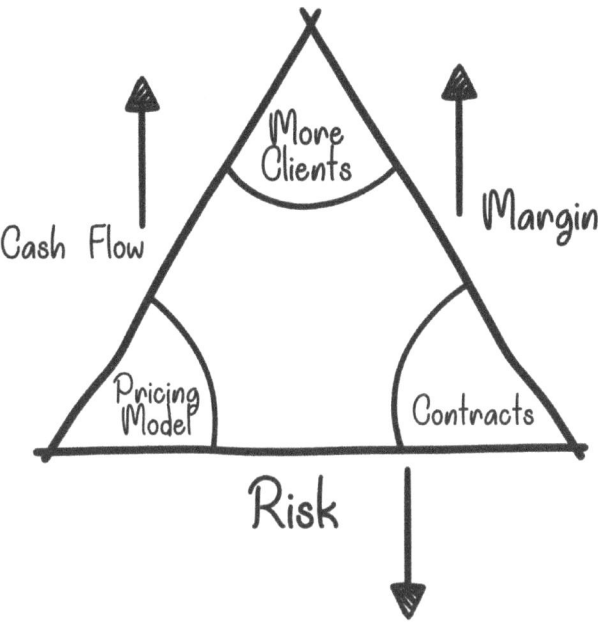

Inside the triangle, on the bottom left, we have the pricing model. To improve cashflow, we need to increase our number of clients and refine our pricing and business model. More clients lead to better cashflow because there are more projects, more clients, and more margin.

We also need to focus on contracts. Contracts can account for anywhere between 5% and 15% of your margin. That's money you could lose if you don't understand the terms or don't know how to manage your contracts.

Remember, **'the returns are in the terms'**, and effective post-award management ensures you get paid for changes and delays while avoiding disputes.

At the bottom of the triangle, the most important factors for reducing risk are pricing, your model, and contracts. If you negotiate to get paid more upfront, the risk of going out of business decreases because you'll have more cash on hand.

When it comes to contracts, the amount of risk that main contractors push down to you is often absurd. They know it. The initial contract is like the first offer from a car salesperson – they don't expect you to accept it without negotiation.

If you accept all the terms as is, you're taking on significant risk. You're essentially putting your company on the line with every project.

One major issue could determine whether your business survives or just faces a small setback. Contracts are crucial for managing risk in the short, medium, and long term.

This book will guide you through each of these elements in detail. Keep reading, and everything will start to make sense. This model keeps you focused on the three biggest levers that increase margins, reduce risk, and improve cashflow. It's easy to remember, and you can print it out to remind yourself and your team what to focus on.

For nearly two decades, I've worked with main contractors and contract owners. I've seen the most successful companies repeatedly use these principles, which I've distilled into this model to make them easy to understand and remember. It simplifies the financial aspects of your construction business.

This model isn't about every detail of construction. It's about the money-making side. Whether you are in scaffolding, civil, or steel fabrication, you might think, *My trade is more complex than this model shows.*

This book doesn't cover how to deliver the best-quality work. It's focused on making money and staying in business for a long time. Of course, delivering quality work is the foundation of this model. Without quality, it won't work.

But if you are delivering quality, this model will help you build a better reputation, feel more secure, and stay in business long-term. You might even pass the business on to your kids or sell it for a great price.

The old process

Let's walk through the old process that most subcontractors follow.

First, they go to the market. They check tendering and bidding websites and reach out to companies to get invited to bid on projects. They get asked to give a bid.

Then, they prepare their bid, which is not cheap to do. Estimating the work and preparing all the necessary documentation takes time, money, and effort – and more often than not, you don't win the project.

When bidding competitively, companies often avoid negotiating the contract terms in the rush to offer the lowest price. This leads to signing risky contracts, as the client typically designs the terms, pushing most of the risk onto you.

If anything goes wrong on the project, they're covered, but you'll bear the brunt of the issues.

If everything goes well and you win the project, it's often at a cost – your margin is low because you had to commoditise yourself to get the job. Essentially, you're just like everyone else, winning work based on the lowest margin.

Many companies often try to negotiate terms after winning a project. This is a mistake, and is one of the quickest ways to frustrate your client and start the project off on the wrong foot.

In many cases, companies haven't even fully read the contract they signed. If they requested changes to the contract, they may not have ensured those changes were reflected in the final version. Our data from over 7000 reviews shows that nearly half the time, all the changes you agreed aren't implemented.

Once the contract is signed, there's a kickoff meeting, typically run by the main contractor. The client is there, and they go over technical details. Often, you're left with a long to-do list before the project even begins. Nothing is mentioned about anything commercial.

At the start of the project, most people value the relationships highly and don't want to cause friction by submitting notices for changes or delays right away. They may try to handle things on-site or combine all the changes into one large request later, thinking it simplifies the process for both sides. I'll explain in a later chapter why this rarely works out.

As the project progresses, delays and changes accumulate, and relationships begin to strain. You haven't been paid for work you should have been, or you've been delayed but haven't submitted the proper paperwork for the delays.

It starts to look like you're at fault. At this point, companies often switch to a more contractual approach, involving lawyers, which adds pressure to already stressed relationships and often causes them to break down.

At the end of the project, during the final payment, clients may withhold payment or try to negotiate a lower amount. They know they owe you, but they may be short on cash as the project wraps up. They may blame your late documentation as a reason to underpay your final claim.

As of writing this book we are facilitating a dispute resolution for a client who has been off site since October 2024. Their final progress claim is being held back to the tune of more than $467,000. Not their retention, their final progress claim.

In the end, you've made little to no margin, and you're back at the starting line, ready to repeat the process.

Over the years, this cycle continues, and it feels like you're going nowhere fast. It all depends on how each project plays out and the reliability of each client – factors over which you have little control.

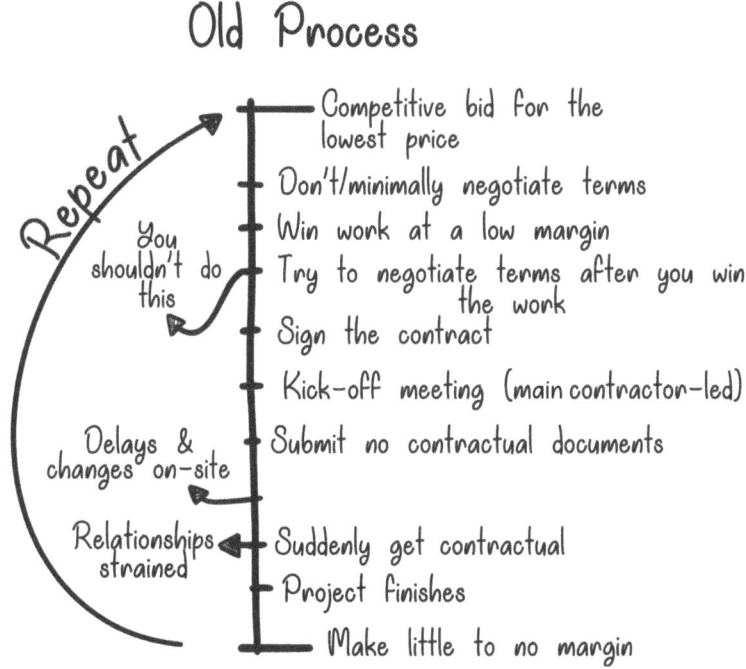

The Quantum Contract System

Let's walk through what I call the 'Quantum Contract System'.

You'll start by bidding competitively at the lowest price, just like before. However, this time, you will negotiate the terms upfront to ensure changes and delays are accounted for in the post-award phase.

You'll get paid for these changes and delays, and ideally, you'll earn a good margin from them as well.

You'll win the work with a low margin but secure an upfront payment. This will boost your cashflow, giving you breathing room and allowing you to run a more efficient project.

Before signing the contract, you will double-check that all agreed changes have been included. If they haven't, you will go back and get the contract updated.

Next comes the kickoff meeting – but this time, you'll lead it. You'll set the agenda and be in control. (We'll cover this in detail in a later chapter.) You'll also set up four check-in meetings, with the goal of establishing a long-term relationship, eventually leading to a framework agreement.

Once the project starts, you'll handle all paperwork related to changes and delays from day one, and follow through on your scheduled check-ins. (We'll dive deeper into these check-ins later.)

One of these meetings will focus on an upsell to a framework agreement, which you aim to have signed by the end of the project. That framework agreement will open the door to new projects with this client.

When you have proven yourself, you can secure better margins and build a stronger relationship with the client.

Clients value good relationships with reliable subcontractors and suppliers. They'll come to you first for new projects because they trust you and already have a signed agreement in place.

With this, you'll enjoy better margins and a stronger reputation.

By the time the project finishes, you'll have higher margins, better cashflow, and less risk. You'll also have set yourself up for more future projects with that client.

Over time, you'll be able to move away from competitive bidding and rely more on your established relationships. This shift is essential to building a proper business system that acts as its own sales process.

In the typical approach, you win one project at a time, moving from job to job. Most people know that if they can get their foot in the door, they can secure more work.

The Quantum process takes this concept further by creating a system where winning one project leads to the potential of winning three or four more.

It multiplies the value of your effort. Since tendering costs money, this system makes the most of that investment, yielding three to four times the return on your tendering efforts.

Quantum Contract System

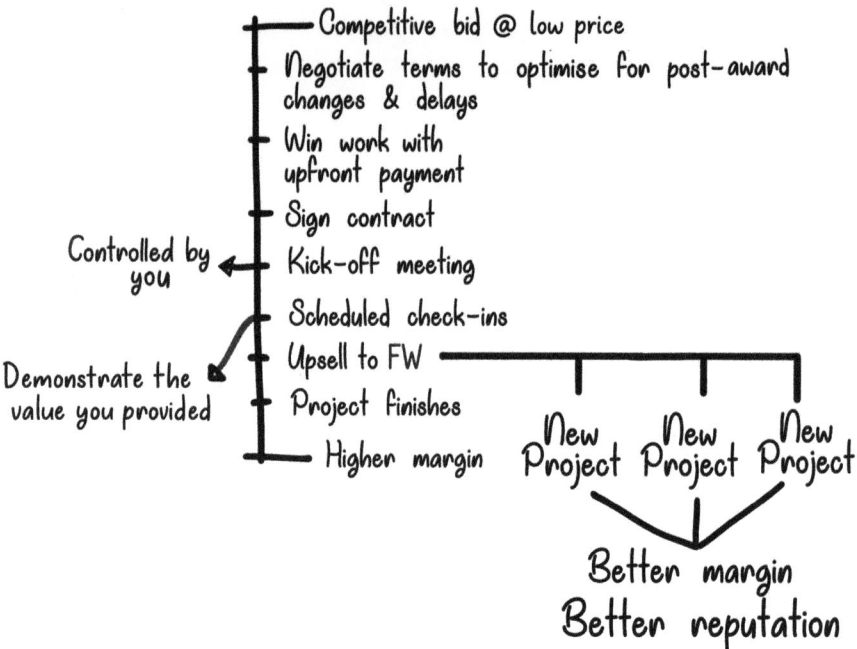

CASE STUDY: FRAMEWORK AGREEMENTS

Accex Scaffolding faced a tough situation on a project. The main contractor went out of business and left them unpaid for over $1.5 million. They had no way to recover the loss.

They couldn't handle another blow like that and were tired of dealing with shaky main contractors.

At the same time, they won another project with a main contractor who had a great reputation, lots of work, and had been around for a long time. It was a very lucky win.

For the new project, they used the Quantum Project Process and got the client to agree to a framework agreement.

To this day, they continue to get repeat work from that client, and they've completely turned things around. They're out of financial pressure and thriving.

You need to shift from a project-based process, driven by competitive bidding, to a system-based approach.

You might be wondering, *When can I switch to this system? I already have ongoing projects – some ending, others just starting. When's the right time?*

Once you understand the system in detail, you can apply it to whatever phase your project is in. Since the system starts by pricing low to win work, you likely already have that part covered.

Take a look at the diagram of the new project process and get familiar with it. Don't skip any steps.

In this book, I'm giving you everything you need to implement this system in your business. I'm not going to sugarcoat it: if you keep relying on competitive bidding, you'll be stuck on a hamster wheel.

You won't grow your construction company or improve your margins. If you want more time with your family or a better reputation in the industry, it won't happen with the current model.

Switch to the new system and you'll see real change.

> ### ACTION ITEM: QUICK WINS
>
> **Step 1:** Right now, review one active project's contract. Check if there are any unaddressed opportunities to submit change or delay requests. If so, document and submit them immediately to start securing extra margin.
>
> **Step 2:** Reach out to one existing client you have worked with more than once and propose a framework agreement for future work.
>
> You are reaching out to your clients so you can avoid having to negotiate terms, delaying getting started and costing everyone money. Get it done once. It'll save them lots of time. Position it so it's a benefit to them.
>
> This will move you away from competitive bidding and help secure long-term relationships.
>
> **Why:** These quick actions – submitting changes for an ongoing project and proposing a framework agreement – can help you start improving cashflow, reducing risk, and building stronger client relationships today.

Chapter 3
The psychology of pricing

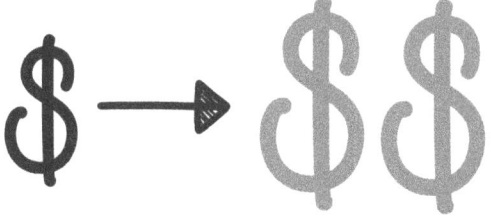

Chapter 3 summary

In this chapter, we explore how to elevate your business from providing budget services to becoming a premium service provider.

You'll learn the mindset and strategies needed to market yourself as a premium option and how to structure your business and pricing to reflect the high value you offer.

This approach not only enhances your margins but also strengthens your reputation in the industry.

Highlights

- Why raising your prices will increase your credibility and attract higher-quality clients.
- How to market your services as premium without alienating your current customer base.
- How to structure your bids to win at the lowest price but still maintain premium standards.
- Why perception of quality is often tied to higher pricing and how to leverage this psychology.

The psychology of pricing

'Price is what you pay. Value is what you get.'

Warren Buffett

Why premium pricing works

Delivering a premium service and getting paid for it puts you on the path to better margins and a stronger reputation in the industry.

This chapter will guide you from where you are now to where you want to be – without losing business in the process. I'll explain why positioning yourself as a premium service provider is critical and how to market yourself as one.

You'll learn how to get clients to recognise your value and be willing to pay for it. However, to get there, you may still need to win bids by offering the lowest price upfront. But that's just the starting point.

↓ Price	Your Clients	Price ↑
Decrease	Emotional investment	Increase
Decrease	Perceived value	Increase
Decrease	Results	Increase
Increase	Demand	Decrease
Decrease	Revenue for fullfilment per customer	Increase

I've already explained the concept of premium versus volume services. In chapter 2, I outlined the old process and the new one for moving forward.

↓ Price	Your Business	Price ↑
Decrease	Profit	Increase
Decrease	Perceived value of self	Increase
Decrease	Perception of impact (results)	Increase
Decrease	Service levels	Increase
Decrease	Sales team conviction	Increase

Credit: Alex Hormozi $100M Offers

You can't simply increase your prices to boost cashflow and margins. You need to follow a process, and this chapter is about that process.

Reputation is everything in the construction industry. As Warren Buffett famously said:

> It takes 20 years to build a reputation and five minutes to ruin it. If you think about that, you'll do things differently.

Your image matters, and your actions shape how others view you. Building trust through consistency and delivering on your promises is crucial. **However, your ability to maintain a reputation for quality work depends on being paid enough to sustain it.**

Let me repeat – your ability to maintain a reputation for quality work depends on being paid enough to sustain it.

Imagine if you made an extra 10% to 15% margin on last year's revenue. What better equipment, materials, or people could you have afforded? How would that improve your peace of mind?

If your clients saw these improvements, how much better would they perceive your business? Premium pricing not only builds your reputation but also keeps your business sustainable. Potential clients respect higher prices because they associate them with better service.

This concept ties into what psychologist Robert Cialdini discusses in his book *Influence: The psychology of persuasion*. People often assume that more expensive products are of higher quality.

You want to position your business this way. Price is a quick indicator of value – people see expensive items as more prestigious and linked to status. Marketing enhances this by promoting high-priced, expert-recommended products, which makes them seem even more valuable.

Additionally, the scarcity of expensive items makes them more desirable, triggering a fear of missing out on something special. When people purchase expensive products, they tend to feel more satisfied to avoid buyer's remorse.

This idea, known as post-purchase satisfaction, increases loyalty to high-priced brands. The higher price signals higher quality and makes the product more desirable, fostering brand loyalty.

So, being seen as expensive should not be a concern. As Cialdini highlights, it's actually an advantage – even beyond the direct benefits to your margins and cashflow.

Pricing itself becomes a tool to drive growth and allow you to take on fewer, more profitable projects.

Let me share a story from my personal life to really drive this point home. Consent to include this story was loosely given over a few glasses of wine.

A few years ago, I was on a holiday in Italy with my wife, her sister Jessica, and my now brother-in-law. It was supposed to be a relaxing vacation, but it turned into an epic hunt for the perfect engagement ring.

Jessica had been dreaming about this ring for months. She knew exactly what she wanted – down to the shape, size, and even the tiniest details of the diamond.

Everywhere we went, she had pictures on hand, showing us her vision. As we travelled from city to city, our leisurely walks through the cobblestone streets turned into a mission. If there was a jeweller in sight, we were in there, searching for the elusive ring.

We scoured Florence, Milan, and Rome, stopping at one high-end jeweller after another. Each time, the same scene played out: we'd step into the shop, Jessica would browse, hopeful, but nothing was quite right.

The perfect ring seemed like a mirage – always just out of reach. Weeks went by, and honestly, we were all starting to think we'd never find it.

Then, we arrived in Venice. Tired but still determined, we wandered into yet another small jewellery shop. And there it was. As soon as we walked in, Jessica's eyes lit up. She knew.

She practically sprinted to the display case, pointing at the ring with excitement. 'That's it!' she exclaimed. It was exactly what she had been searching for – the shape, the size, everything.

She slipped it on, and it fit like it was made for her. The search was over. We were all relieved – and thrilled.

But then, we asked the price. The jeweller smiled and said, 'It's €1000.'

My brother-in-law and I glanced at each other, both thinking he had just hit the jackpot. After all the searching, she had found the perfect ring for a fraction of what we expected.

This was a steal! My brother-in-law was already imagining the money he'd save.

But Jessica's face fell. She hesitated, then handed the ring back. 'I'm sorry, but it needs to be at least 10 times that price,' she said.

Those were her actual words.

We were stunned. The ring was exactly what she had wanted, but to her, the low price tag didn't match the value she associated with such an important purchase. The ring was perfect, but it was too cheap for her to believe it was the right one.

This story perfectly illustrates how price reflects perceived quality. Even when the product was flawless, the price made it seem less valuable in her eyes.

The Subcontractor's Edge

You might be thinking, *If I raise my prices, will clients think I'm charging too much?*

You want to position yourself as premium, but not so expensive that you're out of reach. Finding that balance is key, and the best way to start is by raising your prices to a level that makes you a bit uncomfortable. That's where you'll find the sweet spot.

You want to be expensive, but not ridiculous and unattainable or out of reach. Only you can figure out what that is.

> **EXERCISE: A LIGHTHEARTED PRANK**
>
> At your next work party or even a gathering at home, try this lighthearted prank. Find an unsuspecting victim – ideally the loud, confident type – and set the stage.
>
> Grab three whiskey glasses and mark one with a red sticker, one with a yellow, and one with a blue. The stickers are just to throw them off.
>
> Behind the scenes, fill each glass with the same whiskey. Then, tell them that one is from a $20 bottle, another is $75, and the last is a high-end $150 whiskey. Ask them to guess which is which and explain their reasoning.
>
> Sit back and enjoy as they go on about the different flavours, aromas, and complexities – without realising all three glasses are identical. When they're finished, reveal the punchline.

How buyers make their decisions

Let's take a look at how buyers make their decisions. First, they hear about you – maybe through a referral, word of mouth, or a Google search.

Then they check your website, not to find out what services you offer – they already know that – but to see proof that you can deliver results. They want to know if you finish projects on time and within budget.

Your website should have a clean, professional design that's easy to navigate. Make sure visitors can quickly find what they need and know what to do next. Include a short video explaining who you are, what you do, and how you help your clients.

Back this up with case studies that prove your claims. Your marketing should focus on results, not just services. Highlight key data like '97% on time and on budget', and include client testimonials praising your work, your responsiveness, and how easy it was to collaborate with you. Case studies of successful projects will further demonstrate your expertise.

While your website can briefly mention your services, it should focus primarily on the results you deliver.

Using marketing to promote your premium service

Bad Marketing

1. Focus on:
   You
   Your services
   Techno babble

2. You saying:
   "You're great"

3. No clear:
   "What to do next"

Good Marketing

1. Focus on:
   Results
   Quality
   On time
   On budget

2. Other people saying:
   "You're great"

3. Clear:
   "What to do next"

All your marketing going forward must emphasise your premium service. In construction, this means focusing on on-time completion and staying on budget.

You need to present yourself as a premium provider in everything you do – from your in-person interactions to your marketing materials, including your website. This doesn't mean you need a fancy website, but your messaging must clearly demonstrate that you can deliver high-quality work, on time, and on budget.

Your marketing isn't about being the cheapest upfront, but showing that, in the long run, you provide the best value. You don't need to say this outright, but that should be the core message.

The best way to approach this is to market your results.

What do your clients gain from working with you? They want their projects completed on time, within budget, and without hassle. They want you to be reliable, responsive, and easy to deal with.

But instead of saying all of this yourself, it's more powerful when others say it for you. No one likes a bragger, so the key is getting your clients to do the bragging on your behalf.

Improving your proposals and bid submissions

Your proposals and bid submissions should follow a similar approach. It's all about what should be included and what should be left out.

Again, don't focus too much on the details of what you do – focus on your results. Highlight when you've been on budget, on time, and easy to work with. Structure your proposal so that, before they see your price, they first read about your successes, client testimonials, and past wins. This shows your experience and credibility.

However, keep in mind that most people won't read every word. They'll skim through.

Imagine you're flipping through your own proposal – would the key points stand out?

If they're not going to read long paragraphs, they'll focus on bold text and headings. Test it yourself: can you scan your proposal and still see that you're on time, on budget, and proactive? Does the message come across clearly before they get to your pricing? That's your litmus test.

People do judge by appearance. You could provide the best service, but if your proposals or marketing materials don't look the part, people will judge you poorly on that.

You must be perceived as high-quality, on time, and on budget.

You might think, *It'll be expensive to redo all my marketing.* But it's easier and more affordable than you realise. There are many low-cost service providers who can help you create a professional, clean, and simple website or proposal.

You need to see this as an investment in future profit. Once it's done, it's done. Forget about fancy logos or complicated branding – what matters is that your material looks professional and clean. The content is then key.

The process is simple: build a system within your company to collect case studies, quotes, and client reviews. Have your managers take responsibility for this. You could even give them a KPI to complete a case study and get a positive client quote after each project.

Create a mandatory questionnaire for your project managers to fill out at the end of every job. This ensures you get all the information you need to showcase your results.

Your project managers might feel awkward asking clients for a case study or feedback, but they can easily reframe it: 'Our company requires this at the end of every project to improve our systems. Would you mind filling out this feedback form?'

This way, it feels like part of the process, not a personal request.

Building strong, respectful, long-term relationships

So, how do you become a premium provider while still winning with the lowest bid? The key is to build your business around strong, respectful relationships and gradually move away from competitive bidding.

First, you win a tender with a low bid that covers your costs, allows for mistakes, and provides a small profit. From there, you'll make up your margin in the post-award phase. It's essential to negotiate specific items during the contract phase to set yourself up for success (this will be covered in the next chapter).

Over time, your goal is to build relationships with clients, so you won't have to rely on competitive bidding in the future. Of course, this depends on consistently delivering exceptional results on-site.

In the old process, you would win a competitive bid, complete the project at a low margin, and then start all over again. With the new approach, you can win future projects at higher margins, and the need for competitive bidding decreases over time.

If you've been in construction long enough, you've probably heard of companies 'buying' projects. This usually happens during downturns to cover costs and avoid laying off staff.

Another reason is to build relationships and secure extra work over time. These companies understand that every project will encounter changes and delays – that's where they make their money.

By proving their reliability and ability to deliver, they position themselves to win future work from the same clients.

You might be thinking, *I need to win bids at any cost. This sounds risky.*

But from a pricing standpoint, there's no significant difference between this approach and what you've been doing. You've always bid low to win the job anyway, so the risk hasn't changed.

However, you do need to be more selective about the clients you work with. Choose clients who are financially secure and have a solid reputation for making payments on time. You also want clients who have multiple projects that can offer you long-term work.

There's an old adage in business:

> If you want a better business, get better clients.

I couldn't agree more. At this stage, the only change in your process is selecting the right clients.

Competitive bidding is costly, and since your strategy now is to move away from it, you'll spend less on it in the long run.

The psychology of pricing

> **PRO TIP: REMOTE WORKERS**
>
> A big problem is the cost and effort of preparing a bid. Many times clients will only be 'market testing' to gauge the waters for the average price. It's very annoying but part of the game.
>
> To reduce your costs, consider hiring remote workers. The costs are lower, but the skill level remains high. You can train them in your process, and the upfront time investment will pay off in the long term.
>
> Clear accountabilities, expectations, and training are key to success.
>
> In addition, they may be in a different timezone to you. So you can give them a task at 4.59 pm and it's done when you get into work in the morning.
>
> This will make your bid process more efficient and affordable.

Submitting an alternative bid

Remember, we're shifting the business model to improve cashflow. Submit an alternative bid that includes a request for upfront payment in exchange for a discount on the total price.

This can be part of the proposal process. Justify the request by explaining why you need the upfront payment and how it benefits the client. Assure them that their payment will secure your equipment, materials, and workforce, allowing you to deliver better results and offer a discount. It's an attractive offer for the client.

But remember, you'll still submit your regular bid in case this strategy doesn't fit. The goal is to improve cashflow and make up your margin after the award.

What if you can't make up your margin in the post-award phase? Don't worry – we'll cover that in the rest of this book.

Remember, the returns are in the terms, and the margin is in the post-award phase. Follow the process, and don't be afraid to try it. If the client doesn't want to go along with it, they'll simply ignore it, and you'll still have your regular bid in place.

> **CHAPTER 3 ACTION ITEM: SUBMIT AN ALTERNATIVE BID WITH UPFRONT PAYMENT REQUEST**
>
> **Action:** For your next bid, submit an alternative proposal that includes a request for upfront payment in exchange for a discount on the total price. This should be done in addition to your regular bid to give the client two options. In your proposal, clearly explain why the upfront payment is needed and how it will benefit both parties. Show that receiving the payment upfront ensures better cashflow, allows you to secure materials and labour, and ultimately results in a better service for the client.
>
> **Why:** This strategy improves your cashflow and positions you as a proactive, reliable subcontractor. By offering an upfront payment option, you reduce financial strain, making your business more sustainable, and offer the client a clear benefit – an early discount in exchange for financial security on your end.

Chapter 4
The silent risk

Chapter 4 summary

In this chapter, you'll learn why negotiation is a critical aspect of running a successful business. I'll show you how to approach contract conversations with confidence, reduce your risk, and set up your project for long-term success.

By focusing on key terms and making negotiation a priority, you'll gain respect from clients and improve your financial outcomes.

Highlights

- Why negotiating contract terms builds credibility with clients.
- How to effectively negotiate changes before signing the contract.
- The 'semi-submissive' approach.
- Why avoiding unnecessary legal jargon makes your negotiation more effective.

> 'In business, you don't get what you deserve, you get what you negotiate.'
>
> Chester L. Karrass

How avoiding negotiation can cost you more than you think

You might think you can't negotiate, but you can – and you must. The key is knowing *how* and *what* to negotiate. This is what separates appearing difficult from being professional.

Typically, the client will give you their terms to agree to as part of the bid process.

If you are dictating the contract terms, usually these will be on smaller jobs. My advice is to spend the money on a lawyer to get your terms drafted favourably to use going forward.

You must flag any terms you disagree with at the outset. You cannot negotiate after winning the bid. Negotiating means reading their proposed contract carefully, then responding with your suggestions for changes that will allow you to deliver your premium service. I'll explain exactly what and how to negotiate in this chapter.

You may have been taught that not negotiating makes you seem agreeable. In reality, it can make you look inexperienced. When you negotiate, there are three major benefits:

- **It builds trust.** They'll have more confidence in your ability to do the job. It signals that you've been here before and know what you're doing.
- **You reduce your risk.** A well-negotiated contract protects you from unnecessary risks.

- **You set yourself up for post-award success.** Negotiating early positions you to make more money as the project progresses.

Having been on the other side of the table, I know how this plays out. I used to have KPIs for awarding a certain number of contracts in a year.

Often, we'd have five bidders for a particular scope of work. Of those five, four would negotiate the terms, and one wouldn't bother. The one who didn't negotiate didn't come across as agreeable or easy to deal with. Instead, it was a red flag. It made them seem inexperienced – maybe their first time at this level of project. Not negotiating shows they may not fully understand the game.

Let me share a real example. One of my clients specialised in building noise walls – those structures along highways that block sound from reaching nearby homes.

This client said, 'I don't want to negotiate because I don't want to seem difficult.'

They had two bids in progress at the time. One was for an existing client, and the other was for a new client.

To test the different approaches, we let them handle the bid for their existing client since they felt confident about winning that one. I stepped in to handle negotiations for the new client.

The result? The new client came back and said, 'Thank you for your professionally worded negotiation document. It gave us confidence that you know what you're doing.'

Not only did they win the project, but they also did so with much lower risk than the project won through the existing client relationship. The higher-risk project, based solely on the existing relationship, ended up yielding far less profit.

The lesson here is clear: **if you don't negotiate, they won't respect you.** They will assume you don't understand the process. However, when you negotiate, it gives them confidence that you know what you're doing and you're someone who can be relied on.

Understanding how the other side views you

Understanding how the other side views you during negotiations is crucial to winning a project and delivering a fantastic result. The key is understanding their process.

The person sitting across from you has a KPI to get multiple contracts awarded by a certain deadline. Your job is to make it easy for them to do theirs while still securing the contract terms that work for you.

In most companies, there is a contracts administrator, manager, or someone responsible for awarding 20 to 30 contracts for a given project. If they hit their KPI, they're happy. If they get delayed because of complicated negotiations, they aren't.

These contract experts are often lawyers, construction industry veterans, or contract specialists. They handle this process daily. They prequalify four to six firms, invite them to bid, and then coordinate feedback from several subject matter experts – legal, technical, health and safety, quality – before awarding the contract to the lowest-priced qualified bidder.

Their KPI is to get that contract awarded on time, despite having to manage input from several departments.

What they fear most is awarding a contract and then having the subcontractor come back with a list of changes. If this happens, they have to go back through legal and other departments, delaying the process.

This frustrates them, creates delays, and starts the relationship on a bad note. A good day for a contracts person is getting everything signed off quickly.

If your requests are clear and reasonable, they'll likely approve them to avoid delays. If your requests are too complicated or unclear, they might reject them simply because it's too much hassle.

I've been in this position. With multiple contracts on the go, the easiest requests to understand get approved quickly. Anything too complex or requiring legal review slows down the process.

When I was younger, I would work overtime to get changes sorted, but as I became more experienced, I became less patient. Contractors who made things difficult missed out on big projects, from skyscrapers to oil and gas plants, simply because they didn't make it easy for me to do my job.

You might be thinking, *Isn't it their job to review everything and get back to me if they don't understand?*

Technically, yes. But remember, they're human too. They have family, priorities, and pressures – just like you. And at the end of the day, you want the outcome, so it's in your interest to make the process as easy as possible.

So, change your perspective. The person reviewing your bid is under pressure, just like you. They want to get contracts awarded and move on to the next task.

Your job is to make the fewest, but most impactful, changes to the contract. Keep things clear and simple and you'll build a reputation as someone who makes their life easier.

> **KEY POINT: THE LEAST NUMBER OF CHANGES**
>
> Suggest the least number of changes you can, but ensure those changes have the biggest impact on protecting your business.
>
> If you do that, they'll say 'yes' more often.

How to negotiate successfully

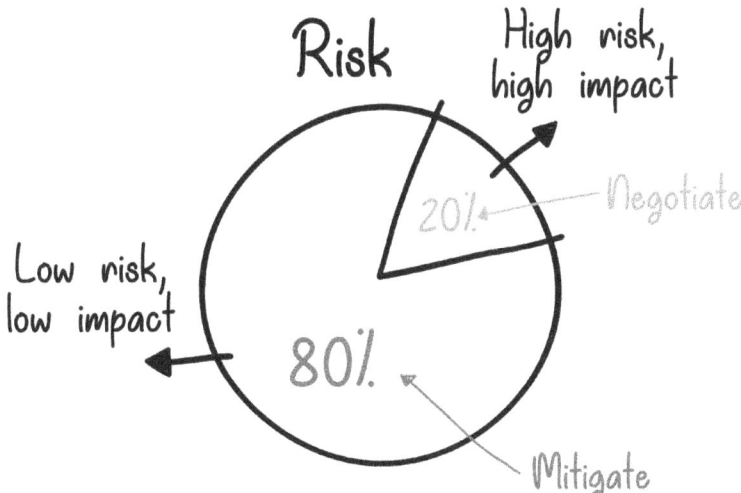

Ultimately, you want to negotiate as little as possible, but what you negotiate must matter to your business and you must negotiate hard for those items.

I've found that when lawyers review construction contracts, they often assess every risk and try to negotiate all of them. The problem with this is the more changes you propose, the less likely you are to get favourable outcomes.

Focusing on just the major items that impact your business will make the other side more willing to negotiate.

A lawyer might prepare a document with a long list of risks that need to be changed, but then *everything* gets rejected.

Lawyers love to suggest changes – I once spent 45 minutes deciding on the definition of the word 'claim' for the definitions section of a contract.

I care because when something goes wrong and there is a claim, everything hinges on that one line of text. The lawyer cares because they get paid per hour to debate this.

The main contractor and subcontractor in the room? They didn't care.

Besides arguing over definitions on page one, there were essentially so many changes to the document that it didn't resemble the original even slightly.

Most of the changes are complex legalese and not applicable to the real-life world of construction.

We ended up throwing out the marked-up version of over 200 changes, working it down to the things that mattered, and settled on 11 changes both parties were happy with.

The lawyer wasn't looking at what the risk was and couldn't weigh what an important change was versus something that didn't move the needle.

If you go to the main contractor with 100 changes, they are going to tell you to get lost. Give them the needle movers, the money makers. Highlight the things that matter.

The reality is, contracts contain different kinds of risks. Depending on your business, some risks may never happen, so is there a point in negotiating those?

Some terms – like some insurance provisions or payment on account – the main contractors will have internal policies to never move on. Is it worth your time to push on something you know they'll never agree to?

There are other risks where the impact on your business is minor, so again, is it worth negotiating?

Then, there are the key risks that could significantly impact your cashflow, reputation, or ability to complete the project. These are the ones you need to focus on. If we know that only a few changes will get through, it's better to negotiate the ones that will make the most difference to your business staying profitable and protecting your margins.

The goal is to reduce risk and position yourself for better margins and cashflow, not to eliminate every single risk. If you try to negotiate everything, you won't achieve much. It's better to concentrate on a few critical issues.

When I was on the other side of the table, I once received a contract negotiation document with over 50 proposed changes. It was obvious the lawyer didn't understand construction.

My first reaction was to send it straight to our legal team. Then I called them and asked what they wanted me to do. Their response was simple: reject them all.

This is why it's crucial to propose as few changes as possible, but focus on the ones that will have the biggest impact.

You might be thinking, *What if a risk I didn't negotiate actually happens?*

Firstly, if you were not negotiating at all before now ... *really?*

Secondly, the strategy here is about reducing your overall risk. By focusing on the major risks, you're protecting your company from the big, business-ending threats.

Yes, some risks will remain, but you'll be in a much safer position overall.

During the bidding process, they will often provide a document where you can propose changes. If they don't, create your own to submit with your bid.

Accept some of the smaller risks, and get the major ones negotiated. It's important to know what these are for your company.

This 80/20 approach will significantly reduce your overall risk. Make it easy for the contract person to approve, and you'll be in a much better position.

The semi-submissive approach

At the time of writing, Quantum has done over 7000 contract negotiations and – through lots of trial and error – perfected the approach of how to negotiate. We know what works, and I'm going to give it to you on a bumper sticker.

When you propose changes, we use a semi-submissive approach. You essentially want to approach it as if you are a small company that's a real business. You're a normal business of real people with reasonable limits.

Often when lawyers get involved, they take the approach of 'we are better than you'. It's almost like they're shouting: 'THIS IS OVER THE TOP AND WE WON'T STAND FOR THIS TYPE OF BEHAVIOUR, AND YOU NEED TO CHANGE IT RIGHT NOW.'

What would you do if you were the contract person reviewing the documents? You find 50 changes to the terms, all in a demanding tone.

You'd give them the middle finger.

It creates a bad impression of your company and paints you as difficult and hard to deal with.

Semi-submissive refers to your language; for example, 'we suggest this would be a reasonable change' – not aggressive. This means you keep the contracts expert on your side and give a great impression of your company's approach.

You're reasonable, you're friendly.

Maybe you're thinking, *Won't I look like a small fry if I don't use a lawyer?* Of course you can use a lawyer. I don't mean to rag on lawyers.

But you should instruct them to use this suggested language. A combative approach won't get the results you want. Remember, you get more bees with honey than vinegar.

Structuring your negotiation document

Here's the structure to make it easy for the main contractor's contract person to agree to your changes:

1. **Make your changes easy to find:** List the page number, section number, and heading you are referring to so they don't have to search through the document. Copy and paste the specific text you're not happy with so they can see it without even opening the contract.

2. **Explain why the clause doesn't work for you:** In plain language, provide a reason, ideally, for how it could negatively impact them.

   For example: 'This wording prevents us from securing materials early for the project, which could cause delays or increase costs that are outside of our control.'

3. **Propose new wording:** Suggest alternative wording and explain why it benefits both parties.

   This will allow them to approve the change quickly without involving their legal team. Even small changes can significantly reduce your risk over time.

> **PRO TIP: LEVERAGE THEIR LAWYERS**
>
> In your negotiation document, indicate that you are open to revised wording proposed by their legal team.

4. **Invest in a one-time legal review:** For a one-time cost, consider hiring a construction lawyer to review your toughest contract.

Ask them to create a document called 'commercial principles'. This document outlines your best-case scenarios for key contract terms.

The lawyer can provide recommended wording for future negotiations, which will save you time and effort on every project. It's a small upfront cost but a long-term investment in protecting your business.

What to negotiate: the three key categories

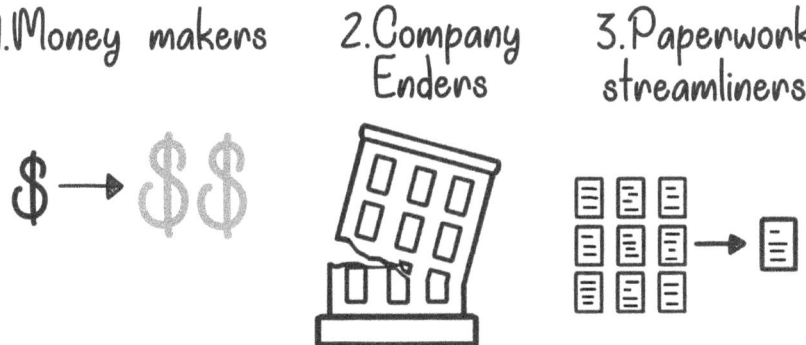

Here's an overview of the three key areas to focus on in negotiations:

- **Money makers:** We'll dive deeper into this in chapter 6, but for now, know that 'money makers' are anything related to payments, changes, delays, or anything else that impacts your cashflow or margins.

    Get these right, and you'll make more money on each project. Get them wrong, and they will cost you.

- **Company enders:** Some contract clauses can sink your entire business if things go wrong. These are the ones you need to keep out of your contracts at all costs.

  Think of it like poker – you don't want to go all-in on every hand. If something goes wrong, you need to make sure it won't take down your entire company.

  By removing these company enders from your contracts, you'll minimise risk and ensure that one bad project doesn't ruin everything.

- **Paperwork streamliners:** Like it or not, paperwork is part of construction. While you'd probably rather be managing your team on-site, contracts often have penalties for late paperwork, like change notifications.

  For example, a contract might say, 'If you don't notify us within two days of a change, you bear the cost.'

  To avoid getting caught out, it's important to negotiate these deadlines and give yourself some breathing room to handle paperwork properly.

  Simplifying the paperwork can save you from unfair penalties, and that's a win for everyone.

These three areas – money makers, company enders, and paperwork streamliners – will help you increase profits, avoid going broke, and handle the worst parts of any project with ease.

> **PRO TIP: WHAT TO NEGOTIATE**
>
> Maybe you don't know what to negotiate.
>
> I could write an entire book just about what to negotiate, but it would probably feel more like a textbook than a business book – and definitely wouldn't be the most fun read.
>
> To make things easier to digest, here's what I've done:
>
> At the end of the book I have provided a chapter called 'Commercial principles'.
>
> In this chapter I lay out:
>
> 1. Each section of the contract that is important.
> 2. What they mean in an easy-to-understand way – no legal jargon.
> 3. Why they are important.
>
> Or you can go to quantumcontracts.com and we'll do it for you.

CHAPTER 4 ACTION ITEM: START NEGOTIATING KEY CONTRACT TERMS BEFORE YOU SIGN

Step 1: Review the contract terms of your next bid closely, focusing on areas that could impact your cashflow, timelines, or risk exposure.

Step 2: Identify two or three critical terms that would have the biggest impact on your business if left unchanged (for example, payment terms or liability caps).

Step 3: Submit a simple, clear request for revisions, explaining why these changes benefit both you and the client. Keep it brief and professional to ensure faster approval.

Why: Negotiating even a few key terms before signing helps protect your business from unnecessary risk and shows clients that you are a professional who understands the process. This approach builds trust while improving your chances of a successful project outcome.

Chapter 5
Setting up long-term wins

Chapter 5 summary

This chapter shifts the way you think about the kickoff meeting, from participating in it to leading it. What used to feel like just a routine task is now your opportunity to take control and begin your new sales process.

By leading the meeting, you're no longer just checking off boxes – you're positioning yourself as a professional and expert, and setting the stage for a long-term relationship.

Highlights

- How and why you need to control the kickoff meeting for project and relationship success.

- Why you need to establish the dominant frame in your client interactions.

- How to structure your new sales process for long-term relationships.

- Why addressing buyer's remorse is critical to ensuring a smooth project start.

> 'He who controls the agenda, controls the outcome.'

Niccolò Machiavelli

Turn the kickoff meeting into the start of your new sales strategy

The purpose of the kickoff meeting is to create an amazing first impression and set yourself up for a long-term relationship with your new client.

Typically, this is the first meeting between you and the client, and it's often organised by them. Usually, they give you an overview of what they want and expect from the project. It's long, repetitive, and mostly about documents, safety standards, and quality control.

When the client runs the meeting, it can quickly turn into a to-do list for you. For example, they might start by asking, 'Where's the XYZ document?', or, 'Have you submitted this yet?', or, 'Have you got this?'

Before you know it, you're on the back foot, bogged down by tasks that take you away from money-making work. Worse, you might leave the meeting with a huge checklist of things to do that aren't crucial to getting the job done.

In addition, regardless of how good you are at your work, you now have created a bad first impression – which isn't your fault.

Another problem is that you might not even have the right people in the room. Often, you're dealing only with the project manager, and you don't get to meet key decision-makers like the project director.

You're just a participant, and the client controls the meeting.

But the kickoff meeting should be different. This is your chance to make a strong first impression – one where you're seen as skilled, in control, and professional. It's the start of your sales process.

Use it to introduce key people, set the agenda, and take charge. Don't be passive. You want to be the one leading the conversation from the very first moment.

Years ago, I was on a large oil and gas project in Iraq. We had a new civil works subcontractor come in for a kickoff meeting.

Our construction manager was aggressive, wanting to set the tone: 'I'm not taking any nonsense from these guys.'

So, he started the meeting with a list of things they hadn't done. The subcontractor was immediately on the back foot. They sat there and took it, without discussing how to do the job or who they needed to talk to.

They weren't in control, and they walked away with nothing but a huge to-do list. They left looking incompetent, and the relationship never recovered.

Even if you have a nice client, you're still at their mercy if you don't take control. This can make you look like you don't know what you're doing, and it sets the stage for a bad working relationship.

This chapter will cover several important topics. First, we'll discuss how to take control of the meeting.

Then, we'll dive into buyer's remorse and why it's critical to understand. Next, we'll go over how to set the agenda and what to include.

Finally, we'll look at how to kick off your sales process and set up opportunities for upselling later in the project.

Controlling the kickoff meeting

You want to control the kickoff meeting to establish your company as the leader. This doesn't mean being aggressive – it means being in charge and in control.

Set up the meeting as soon as possible after winning the bid and before the project starts. By organising it yourself, you decide who attends.

Invite their project manager and the key people your team will work with, but most importantly, invite the project director. They have the power to offer you future work.

You will lead the meeting, present your agenda, and make it clear that this is not just a technical discussion.

It's your chance to show them *your* process. If possible, host the kickoff meeting at your office – your home turf. If that's not an option, book a boardroom near their office.

Frame control

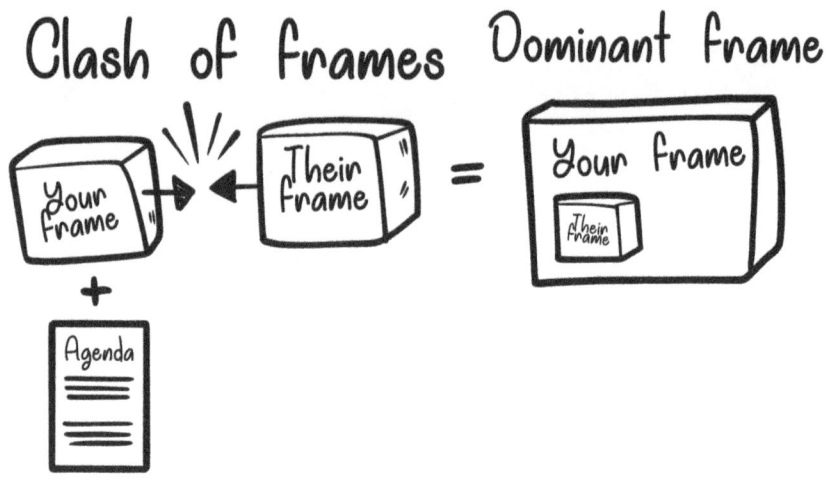

What you're going to be doing is called 'frame control'.

Frame control, a concept from Oren Klaff's book *Pitch Anything*, is the ability to manage the context of social interactions and negotiations.

By controlling the frame, you set the tone, direction, and rules of the conversation, positioning yourself as the authority. This allows you to guide the discussion and manage expectations.

Your goal is to align your client's emotions and thoughts with your objectives. Effective frame control builds confidence, neutralises their concerns about your ability to deliver, and makes you look like you have been doing this for many years.

In any meeting, there's a 'battle of the frames' to see who takes control. You've probably noticed this in previous kickoff meetings, where someone tries to assert dominance.

Whoever sets the frame wins the battle and gains power. Your goal is to win this battle and establish the dominant frame.

By being the dominant frame, you can steer interactions in your favour. You know how to deliver the best outcome for your client, so your ideas and objectives should take priority.

This builds authority and boosts your chances of achieving the desired results. It benefits both you and your client and helps build your reputation.

In this kickoff meeting, you also want to impress the project director, who can offer you future work and help resolve any issues quickly. (We'll dive deeper into this in chapter 7, the dispute chapter.)

Think of it like this:

Imagine you walk into an average restaurant, a pimply teenager seats you and hands you the menu.

You ask the waiter: 'What's good?'

The teenager responds: 'Everything's nice.'

You ask about the wine, and she says: 'Oh, all the wine is good.'

It's a pretty flat experience.

Now imagine you're in a Michelin-star restaurant. The waiters are highly trained, and they don't act like submissive order-takers. They take the dominant frame.

The waiter might say: 'We have a fantastic new dish featuring seasonal vegetables, and we've just gotten in some extra marbled wagyu steak, and if you order that, I highly recommend pairing it with this red wine.'

The waiter has taken control, and suddenly you feel confident in your choice. You think, 'Yes, that sounds amazing!'

The dominant frame creates a better experience. The waiter guides you to the best option for the best experience because that's what they do all day.

That's exactly what you want to do in the kickoff meeting – take control, guide the client, and create the best experience.

I am sure many of you have arrived on site one day, kind of not knowing what to do and where to go, getting onboarded and so on. You still need to meet everyone, figure out the details. It is chaos.

As your business grows, you want to be the waiter at the Michelin-star restaurant.

We have a client with an entirely female leadership team who found project kickoffs quite intimidating. Construction can be a gentlemen's club.

So they flipped the script.

They host the kickoff meeting. They run the presentation. They introduce themselves to everyone and outline the expectations.

The feedback we got from them is that not only does the project go much smoother, they are now acquainted with everyone who matters, the decision-makers, and it is easier to get claims and disputes handled.

They didn't expect respect to be gifted to them. They stood up, made themselves known, and laid out the experience for the client.

Treat your clients like they are diners at your restaurant, introduce yourself, set the expectations, handle any issues quickly and efficiently, and they will keep coming back.

But it all starts with that first experience. Make that kickoff count.

Dealing with pushback

What happens if you get one of these dominant construction manager–types trying to wrestle back control in the meeting?

This often happens with unorganised kickoff meetings. But when you design, set up, and invite people to a well-structured process, you stay in control.

If they start to stray from the agenda, you can bring them back by saying, 'Right, let's get back to the agenda.'

This lets you regain control. If they want to add something before the meeting, let them, but you decide the agenda, its order, and its importance.

By organising the kickoff meeting, they'll actually be relieved you're taking control – it's one less thing on their to-do list.

If a company insists, 'We run the kickoff meetings,' which is rare, just ask, 'Can we add a section for our process to the agenda? That will cover what we're trying to do.'

Later, we'll go over the agenda setup in detail. But for now, know that you should be the one organising the meeting.

You might be tempted to get your project manager to handle this, but as the owner, you should run the meeting yourself.

Even if you typically step back from these interactions, I highly recommend attending this one.

Building a relationship with their project director will benefit you in the long run. Think of this as the start of your sales process for a long-term relationship. This meeting isn't just about project logistics; it's about business development.

Here's a simple email script for setting up the meeting:

> Hi [Project Director's Name],
>
> The success of this project is important to us. As part of our process, we invite new clients to a kickoff meeting at our office to start the relationship on the right foot.
>
> This meeting won't be overly technical. Instead, we'll explain our proven process from past projects, clarify roles, and improve communication to ensure success.
>
> Here are a couple of proposed times and dates for the meeting: [Insert options].
>
> On our side, we will have [List attendee roles]. We'd appreciate it if [List suggested attendees' roles from their side] could join.
>
> Best regards,
>
> [Your Name]
>
> [Your Company]

Handling buyer's remorse

Even though you've won the project and signed the contract, your client might still experience buyer's remorse.

You need to make them feel confident they made the right decision. The key is to close the gap between signing the contract and delivering value.

Remember how we spoke about the Michelin-star experience – what can you do to seal the partnership between contract signing and contract start?

I used to send a bottle of whisky and a handwritten note to the client the same day the contract was signed, letting them know I was excited to work with them.

The other thing to do is set update intervals where you check in with them to see how things are going.

Clients want to feel like they have all your attention. Make them feel that way.

Buyer's remorse happens because every buyer, after making a decision, feels insecure. Their reputation is at stake – if anything goes wrong, it'll be on them. Shortening this period of uncertainty makes a big difference.

They'll have unspoken questions in their mind like:

- **'Do these guys know what they're doing?':** By controlling the frame, you give them the same comfort as a dominant, confident waiter.

- **'Am I going to get value for the price I paid?':** They'll appreciate you taking initiative, like setting up the kickoff meeting and removing tasks from their to-do list.

- **'Was it all talk and no action? Were the shiny proposals just fluff with no substance?':** By organising the meeting, you show that you're different. You have substance. Invite the right people so the client can meet your team, put faces to names, and judge for themselves.

- **'Are they going to be a pain to work with? Will I actually enjoy this?':** Bring a small, thoughtful gift for everyone in the room. It's an old custom, but it's become a lost art.

  If the meeting is virtual, use old-fashioned snail mail. Everyone loves to receive a package.

  People still appreciate the gesture, and there's a specific way to do it. This is not a branding exercise – no company mugs or pens with your logo.

  The gift should be personal and meaningful to them or the project. For example, custom pens or journals with their initials, or something related to their favourite sports team.

> The goal is to make it about them. A personalised gift leaves a lasting impression.

Buyer's remorse is a well-known phenomenon. If you don't address these unspoken concerns, you miss a chance to build trust. Worse, you might even create doubt.

This is about human psychology – people worry by nature. Why not control the situation and put their mind at ease?

Imagine you're the project director for a large construction project with two bridges.

Subcontractor 1 wins the contract, signs it, and you don't hear from them until the kickoff meeting, which you have to run.

You're left feeling like they're disorganised or uninterested, and now you're chasing them for updates. It feels as if now that they have the signature on the contract, they've checked out.

During the meeting, you have to point out what they need to do and where they're already falling behind.

You might be thinking, *Did I make the right choice? Are they going to be difficult to work with?*

Subcontractor 2 wins the second bridge contract, but they take control from the start. They organise the kickoff meeting, set the agenda, and host it at their office.

You meet the team, and they walk you through their process step by step, giving you confidence that they know what they're doing.

You leave with a personalised pen, and it seems that they've considered everything – even the little details.

You're thinking, *These guys have it together. They're going to make this project run smoothly and we are getting value for money.*

Even if both subcontractors charged the same, which one would leave you feeling more confident and comfortable about your decision?

Some might worry about company policies on gifts. In nearly two decades of experience, I've rarely seen any policies that reject small, personalised gifts like a pen with someone's name.

Personalisation is the real value. So, decide on a gift, organise it, and make sure it's ready before the kickoff meeting.

Setting the agenda

The kickoff meeting has two key parts: the process section and the technical section.

In the process section, you set the dominant frame, guide them through your plan, and organise check-ins. Explain why the check-ins are important and schedule them on the calendar (very important).

The technical section covers the obligations of the project – things like safety and quality management plans and other required documents. Each client and project will have different technical needs, so ensure you have a plan for submitting everything on time as per the contract.

It's easy to become bogged down in technical details, so prepare in advance and don't let the meeting get derailed.

When the meeting starts, there will be some chit-chat as people settle in. It's your job to keep things moving and get down to business.

A common mistake is thanking people for attending. This makes you seem 'less than', as if you're lucky they graced you with their attendance.

Instead, use a phrase like, 'It's great we could all carve out some time. We only have an hour, so let's get started.'

This shows you're busy, professional, and ready to lead the meeting.

Now, here's the agenda you'll present on the screen and in a printed handout:

1. Introductions:

Start with everyone introducing themselves, their team, and their role in the project.

2. Escalation matrix:

Show who to contact for any issues – cost, technical, safety, or quality. Make sure to link each project contact to their counterpart to avoid confusion and wasted time.

3. Project check-ins:

This is where you set up your sales process. Explain that you split the project into four sections, with quarterly check-ins with the project director. These check-ins will review progress, discuss improvements, and get feedback.

We'll discuss the 'how to' in detail in chapter 8, but let me give you a brief overview now.

For the first two check-ins, your goal is to show them the quality of your service is undeniable.

In the third check-in, you'll propose a framework agreement.

The fourth check-in is when you aim to get the framework agreement signed.

> **AN IMPORTANT STEP TO REMEMBER: FRAMEWORK AGREEMENTS**
>
> This is very important and something that we will refer back to when we ask to get a framework agreement set up in your third check-in meeting.
>
> After explaining the check-ins, you'll ask the project director:
>
> 'Look, we are committed to doing an excellent job for you. If, at the end of this project, you are happy with the quality of our work, would you be opposed to discussing a framework agreement with us?'
>
> Phrasing it like this makes it easier for them to agree.
>
> You might be thinking: *Isn't it a bit early to bring up a framework agreement?*
>
> Actually, this isn't about pushing for a commitment right away; it's about planting the seed and showing you're focused on building a long-term relationship.
>
> By framing it as *something to discuss if they're pleased with your work at the end of the project*, you're simply opening the door for future collaboration, not rushing into anything.

4. BAMFAM (book a meeting from a meeting):

Before the meeting ends, get your laptops out and schedule the four check-ins right there. Don't leave this step for later.

Lock in the dates as placeholders, even if it ends up being a Zoom call. It's important to get these in the calendar now, especially since senior people's time can be hard to schedule.

5. Contractual section:

Review the contract's key terms around payment, changes, delays, and extra work. Set the expectation that both sides will follow the contract and communicate about these topics as needed.

6. Technical section:

This section covers the necessary technical documents and plans. Most kickoff meetings spend too much time here. That's why we save it for the end – if time runs out, we can always follow up later.

Let them know your submission schedule and reassure them that you're on top of everything.

7. Closing the meeting:

End on a positive note by giving your counterparts a small, thoughtful gift. This reinforces the dominant frame and leaves a lasting impression of professionalism and preparedness.

Since meetings often run out of time, saving the technical section for last ensures that the most critical elements – like check-ins and contractual expectations – are covered first.

After the next meeting is scheduled, send a follow-up email with a summary of the meeting and highlighting the check-in dates.

By owning the agenda, you stay in control of the meeting and the relationship.

> **CHAPTER 5 ACTION ITEM: ORGANISE AND CONTROL THE KICKOFF MEETING**
>
> **What to do:** Immediately after winning your next bid, organise and schedule the kickoff meeting yourself.
>
> Don't wait for the client. Ensure the meeting takes place on your terms, ideally at your office or a neutral, professional venue. This allows you to control the setting and the agenda.
>
> **Why:** Taking control of the meeting from the outset sets you up as the authority, establishes the dominant frame, and positions you to lead the project in a way that aligns with your process and long-term sales goals.

Chapter 6
The secret weapon

Chapter 6 summary

In this chapter, you'll learn how changes and delays can bring both risks and opportunities in construction projects.

You'll discover how the top subcontractors turn these challenges into profits by negotiating key terms before signing contracts and managing them effectively throughout the project.

Mastering this will set you apart in the construction industry.

Highlights

- Why changes and delays are the hidden key to making more profit in construction.
- How to negotiate smarter to ensure you get paid fairly for changes and delays.
- How one simple adjustment can protect you from working for free.
- Why speeding up approvals for changes and delays will save you headaches.
- How submitting changes early and often can avoid cashflow problems.

'In the middle of difficulty lies opportunity.'

Albert Einstein

Using changes and delays to your advantage

Changes and delays are where the best companies make real money in construction. They are also where many average construction companies lose out.

If you master this part, you'll increase your profits on every project.

> **KEY POINT: THE CHANGES AND DELAYS SECTION**
>
> From a money-making perspective, the most important part of negotiating before you sign is the changes and delays section. This is where your potential to increase profits lies.

I'll walk you through exactly what to do after the contract is signed so you can maximise the outcome of those negotiations. If you want long-term success in construction, this is the area you need to master.

Let me share a story about two electrical subcontractors.

I was on a massive project in the Pilbara region of Western Australia in 2012, called in as a dispute expert. This example is almost too perfect to be true. It's almost as if it was designed as a study by researchers – but I promise, this is a real-life situation.

The project was so large that one electrical subcontractor wasn't enough to complete the whole project – so two were hired, working in different areas but with the exact same scope of work.

One company was new to the industry. Their main focus was doing great work, trusting the contracts to fall into place. They believed that as long as they performed well, they'd be rewarded.

The other subcontractor was well-established with a reputation for being professional and contract-savvy.

Which one do you think did better?

The established company did an okay job – nothing exceptional – but they got all their changes and delays approved. As a result, they made substantial money on the project.

The newer subcontractor, on the other hand, did fantastic work. They impressed everyone and were constantly assigned more tasks. However, they were terrible at documenting changes and delays.

By the end of the project, it looked like they were far behind on their original scope, but that wasn't the case at all.

They had been given a lot of extra work, and they completed it. When they submitted their claims for changes, they were rejected for not following the contract's procedures.

They weren't going to be paid for any of the extra work. Worse, they faced liquidated damages (an agreed cost/day) for being late on the original scope.

I was called in to help this subcontractor. While I was able to navigate the dispute and help them avoid going under (which I considered a win given their poor contractual position), they still lost a lot of money on the project.

Mastering the contract

Head to the **changes and delays** section of your contract.

Many successful subcontractors bid low to win jobs, aiming to make up margins through changes and delays. Your goal is to ensure you're paid fairly for these.

However, there are risks. Some contracts require you take all changes and delay responsibility, or they limit your claims to small amounts or specific changes.

Even worse, these changes are often at the client's discretion, leaving you with no control over when or if you'll get paid.

Time bars are another trap. Contracts often require you to notify changes or delays within two days.

Miss that window, and you lose the right to claim, even for valid delays or changes. I've seen subcontractors lose money simply by missing these deadlines, leaving them working unpaid and harming their cashflow.

This is where you win or lose that 15% most of the time. The biggest rejected claim I have seen in 2024 was $824,000 because they missed their 10-day time bar.

They swallowed that cost all at once as they learned their lesson. Since then, across various projects they have recovered close to a million dollars in claims.

The fortune is in the paperwork. Luckily they had the cashflow to weather that storm but not everyone will be so lucky. Learn from their mistakes.

The biggest cashflow hit comes when clients request extra work. It often leads to cost disputes, delaying your payment.

By then, you've probably started the work, paying your crew and buying materials – essentially financing the project for the client.

Four key negotiation points

These four strategies will ensure you get paid faster and at better margins:

- **Negotiate specific changes and delays:** Ensure common changes in your trade are listed and covered.

- **Remove payment limits:** Avoid caps on how much you can claim. Use the term 'demonstrated actual costs', meaning you'll be paid for what you actually incur.

- **Extend time bars:** Aim for five days to notify the client of a change or delay and another five days to submit the paperwork.

- **Set rates for changes:** Agree on predetermined rates for changes to avoid last-minute negotiations. These rates can be higher than your quoted rates, boosting your margins.

Most construction leaders don't know to negotiate these terms, but now you do.

After negotiating more than 7000 construction contracts and managing $30 billion in value, I've seen these terms make the biggest difference.

You might think, *They won't accept these changes.*

But as I cover in the negotiation chapter, they will be more open to it than you expect. If they aren't willing to agree, ask yourself – are you happy doing work for free?

Everyone knows construction projects come with changes and delays. If they're not willing to negotiate, are they really someone you want to work with? Are they someone you can *afford* to work with?

At the bid stage, address these four points. They ensure you'll be paid for changes and delays. If you can't agree, reconsider if it's worth moving forward.

It might feel intimidating the first time you negotiate, but you'll get the hang of it quickly – I promise.

When it goes wrong

You could (hypothetically) negotiate the perfect contract, with all the terms in your favour. But if you don't manage it properly, it's worthless. Most companies mess up their projects because they rely on relationships, not contracts.

They think: *If we do a good job, it won't matter.*

That may have worked in the past, but today that's no longer the case. Relationships often disappear when you need them most.

For example: if you're dealing with a project manager at the end of a two- or three-year project, what do you think he's focused on?

He's likely on job sites looking for his next gig because he knows this project is wrapping up. Often they bring in a closeout team for this exact reason.

Plus, everyone has their own pressures at work, and cutting costs could be one of them. Guess who gets hit by that? You.

How a project normally plays out

Q1
Everyone is happy
Excited
Not concerned about the contract

Q2
Still okay
Some issues
Still not contractual

Q3
Problems
Relationship starting to deteriorate
Some cash flow issues
Threats

Q4
Suddenly get contractual
Relationship gone
Disputes
Lose money
Major cashflow issues

Let's split a project into four stages:

- **Quarter 1:** Everyone's happy. It's a new project, and you're excited to be on-site. People aren't too concerned with the contract yet.

  Small changes happen, and there's a delay or two, but there's plenty of time to catch up. No worries so far.

- **Quarter 2:** Things are still going okay, but issues are creeping in.

  You're still not submitting paperwork when you should, but the schedule still has some flexibility. You're fine taking a hit to keep a good relationship.

- **Quarter 3:** Now, problems are mounting. Relationships are starting to weaken.

  Cashflow is suddenly an issue, and you need to get those changes approved. You're scrambling to remember all the changes and delays, but now you're time-barred.

- **Quarter 4:** Panic mode sets in. You need to get paid to cover your team, but from their side, they know you're in a weak position.

You have minimal leverage in any negotiations. Does this sound like your last project?

This is how things usually play out on a construction project, and it destroys relationships and costs money. The whole model depends on building strong relationships with clients, and the best way to do that is to be **contractual** from the start.

The Subcontractor's Edge

The importance of the final quarter of a project

Let me introduce you to one of my favourite sayings.

> ### SQUEAKY BUM TIME
>
> 'Squeaky bum time' is a phrase coined by legendary Manchester United manager Sir Alex Ferguson.
>
> He used it to describe the tense, nerve-wracking final moments of a football match – or the closing stages of a season – when the pressure is at its highest and every decision counts.
>
> The term perfectly captures the feeling of sitting on the edge of your seat, as both fans and players feel the weight of the game, especially when a title or crucial result is on the line.
>
> The 'squeaking' refers to the sound of people shifting nervously in their plastic stadium seats, anxious about the outcome.
>
> Ferguson first used the phrase during the 2002–03 Premier League season, when Manchester United was in a tight title race with Arsenal. As the games dwindled, small mistakes could make or break a team's entire season.
>
> In these moments, real winners emerge – those who can handle the pressure, stay focused, and seize victory.
>
> It's the ultimate test of mental strength and endurance, where champions are made and seasons are defined.

Construction is the same. Everything goes down in the final quarter.

All disputes and major issues surface because priorities shift. The project, or the client, is often running over budget, and the money isn't there like it was at the start.

You need more money, but you haven't followed the contract, and now you're struggling with cashflow. This is where disputes happen.

The key is knowing how the game plays out and being prepared.

Times have changed

A lot of construction owners might say, 'It's worked for me in the past. We've always worked things out with a handshake.'

But things have changed.

Even smaller companies now have corporate governance systems in place. They have software that requires approval from their side to pay you. One of the boxes that needs to be ticked is: 'Have they complied with their contract obligations?'

If you haven't, they can't pay you – end of story. If just one issue arises where you don't get paid, you can lose your 5% to 10% margin.

Suddenly, you're working for free. To avoid this, enforce your contract from the start using the strategy I'm about to outline.

How to do it the right way

As we discussed, most major issues, disputes, and cashflow problems happen in the last quarter of a project.

By that point, many companies haven't used the right paperwork to protect themselves, and they end up in a bind.

If you start contractually from quarter one, **clients won't think you're difficult.** Instead, they'll see you as professional and respect you.

They'll think: *Oh, these guys have been here before. They know what they are doing, they must have good systems in place.*

I've been on the other side, and this is exactly how it works.

> **KEY POINT: DO NOT WAIT**
>
> Start submitting **small** delays and changes *as they happen*. Do not wait to compile them into a big one.

Doing this builds a solid body of evidence.

When the final quarter arrives, and your clients want to cut costs (as they always do), they won't target you. They'll go after subcontractors who aren't contractually prepared.

If you've followed a system from day one to report changes and delays, your cashflow will improve, and you'll get paid quickly for work you've already done.

In the early stages, clients are more likely to approve changes and pay you because they're not stressed about money yet.

From a leverage point of view, whoever controls the money holds the power. If they've already paid you for small changes, there's less at stake in the final quarter, and you'll be in a much better position.

Test the waters early

Another benefit of starting contractually is that you can gauge how the client handles approvals early on.

Are they approving and paying you quickly?

If you wait until a large change piles up, they might reject it. By submitting small changes and claims early, you get a sense of how responsive they'll be.

If they're slow, you can bring it up early in the project, when the stakes are lower.

You could say: 'You've asked us to make changes, which we are more than happy to do, but it's taking a long time to approve them; we are fine, but it's starting to affect our cashflow.'

This sets the tone, and they may adjust their behaviour. If they don't, you'll know it's not worth making changes for them if they won't pay.

The Subcontractor's Edge

> **PRO TIP: CASHFLOW**
>
> From my experience on both sides of the fence, when you, the subcontractor, raise a fair request and mention that your **cashflow** is being impacted, the bigger company tends to act quickly to fix the issue.
>
> Large companies often get accused of using underhanded tactics with subcontractors, and **cashflow** is the trigger word that gets their attention. They know that if your cashflow is strained, a whole range of problems could follow – problems that could damage their reputation and impact your ability to finish the job.
>
> Just be sure to frame it right: let them know you're okay, but that it's starting to affect your cashflow. That way, you're more likely to get a fast resolution.

CASE STUDY: A COSTLY LESSON

One of the worst stories I've come across is an Australian civil subcontractor who was told by the project manager not to submit changes and delays as they occurred. Construction was built on handshake deals mostly in the past.

What the subcontractor didn't know was that the push to hostile contracting was coming.

The project manager suggested rolling everything into one big claim at the end. Red flag. The subcontractor followed this advice and submitted a $1.5 million claim, which was approved *and paid*.

But when that project manager left, a new one came in. During the final account review, the subcontractor was owed $2.75 million.

The closeout team sent a letter saying: 'That $1.5 million was approved in error. We're offsetting that from your final payment.'

They never got the full amount they were owed, resulting in a huge financial hit. This is why you need to be contractual from day one.

It isn't nice but business isn't nice. Assume if the contract says otherwise that your agreement with a project manager means nothing.

Contractual compliance is king. Even if the project manager tells you to do this, still submit your claims as per the compliance requirements.

Trust me, you will need that body of evidence sooner or later.

You can control when you do the work

Sometimes the contract says: 'You have to get started on the additional work we have instructed, regardless of approval.'

This is a nasty clause that you should try to negotiate out. If you're stuck with it, you can still control when you do the work.

Consider taking a page from nurses in Ireland, who would commence a 'go slow' when they had pay disputes.

Instead of stopping work completely, they'd only do the bare minimum. You can do the same, because if you do walk off site you open yourself to a whole world of problems.

Tell your client, 'Yes, we're doing it, and it's scheduled to be done', but focus on completing the original work as a priority.

This signals to the client that you're willing to comply, but you won't rush into extra work unless the financials are sorted.

Staying on top of changes and delays

Going forward, have a project manager or dedicated person on-site whose sole job is to spot changes and delays that aren't your fault – whether it's client requests, issues with other subcontractors, or the weather.

This person should document these changes, submit the notice within a day or two, and follow up with formal change orders or extension of time requests.

The goal isn't perfection from the start – it's about getting the documents in early. You can always revise them later if needed. The key is to have the paperwork on record.

Many subcontractors make the mistake of assigning this responsibility as a side task to the project manager, who is already too busy.

From my experience, project managers often forget about contracts because they have their hands full elsewhere. But this contractual stuff is where the money is – it's key to better cashflow and margins. Skimping on a dedicated person will cost you more in the long run.

> **GOLDEN TICKET**
>
> At Quantum, this is what we do day in and day out. If it's something you could be interested in, visit **quantumcontracts.com**, book a call and give them this code: thefixfirstmonth for a special discount.

> **CHAPTER 6 ACTION ITEM: START TRACKING CHANGES AND DELAYS FROM DAY ONE**
>
> **Step 1:** On your next project, assign a dedicated person (or yourself) to track any changes or delays as they occur.
>
> **Step 2:** Create a simple log – either a spreadsheet or a document – where you note down each change or delay, the date, and any relevant details.
>
> **Step 3:** Submit the first notice of change or delay within two days of it happening, even if it's minor. This will start building the habit of submitting changes early and often.
>
> **Why:** Doing this from the start will protect your cashflow, avoid last-minute disputes, and help you build leverage for faster approvals, keeping your project on track financially.

Chapter 7
How to avoid disputes

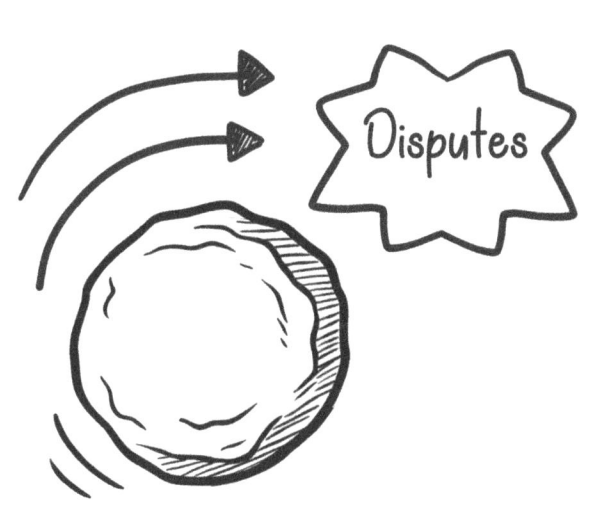

Chapter 7 summary

In this chapter, we dive into the harsh reality of construction disputes – costly, frustrating, and best avoided.

You'll learn how to prevent conflicts from escalating, saving both time and money. By mastering de-escalation and effective negotiation strategies, like the GROW model, you'll stay out of court and protect your business from unnecessary losses.

Highlights

- Why construction disputes are a losing game, even when you 'win'.
- How to de-escalate conflicts before they damage your reputation.
- How to recognise hidden motivations that can strain relationships.
- Use the GROW Model to take control of negotiations and prevent costly disputes.
- Learn a simple conversation tactic to keep the upper hand in difficult discussions.

'An ounce of prevention is worth a pound of cure.'

Benjamin Franklin

How disputes drain cashflow, reputations, and relationships

Here's the thing about disputes: you lose even when you win. And the reality is, you're more likely to lose a dispute than win it.

A dispute is just a race to see who can lose the least amount of money.

Once you get that, you'll realise it's a game you don't want to play. Instead, you want to play the dispute avoidance game.

The three most common types of disputes in construction are:

- **They don't want to pay for work you've done.**

    For example, Jack's steel company finishes a job, but the main contractor refuses to pay the final invoice, citing minor issues that weren't Jack's fault.

- **They ask for extra work but won't pay for it.**

    For instance, Sarah's electrical company installs additional outlets as requested, but when she sends the bill, the main contractor refuses to pay, claiming the extra work was part of the original job.

- **Delays – and who's to blame.**

    For example, Mike's scaffolding company is delayed starting a job due to issues caused by the main contractor. Later, they blame Mike for the project delay and threaten penalties.

In construction, disputes only begin when someone files a claim. Before that, it's just talk – people saying: 'You're not getting paid for this,' or, 'I'll kick you off-site for that.'

A formal dispute has a clear start. It begins when one party submits a dispute notice to the other, which, more often than not, will be you.

Your contract will outline the process that disputes will follow, including the dispute notice. Disputes can be big or small, but either way, your reputation and profits will take a hit. In some cases, it can set your business back five years or even ruin it.

Let me give you an analogy for disputes in construction.

Imagine you're driving, following all the rules, when a car crashes into you at a red light. The driver admits it's entirely their fault. That sounds like a great outcome, right?

But even though it's clearly not your fault, you still come out behind. You'll need to go through insurance, which could raise your premiums.

You'll deal with the hassle of repairs and may need a loan car. Plus, your car's value will drop because it's been in an accident.

So even though you 'won', you still lose.

It's the same in construction disputes. You can be right, win the dispute, and still come out behind.

Often, you'll lose more than you expected. The key is to get ahead of the problem and deal with it before it escalates. Follow this plan to minimise the damage.

The de-escalation conversation

The goal isn't to win disputes. It's to stop conflicts from escalating into disputes in the first place.

If you've applied the strategies discussed earlier in this book, you've already taken steps to prevent disputes.

You'll have a better contract, which reduces disputes. You'll manage changes and delays more effectively, leaving no room for confusion. Regular check-in meetings also give you the chance to address issues early, before they become full-blown problems.

This helps you build a strong relationship with the client's project manager or whoever you're dealing with. For this chapter, we'll assume you're working with the project manager.

Let's consider the project manager's motivations.

They want to impress their project director and avoid blame for any issues. If their work causes delays or disputes, they'll pin the blame on you to protect their career.

They'll do everything to keep problems from reaching the project director. They'll try to make themselves look good, even if that means shifting all the issues onto you.

Because of this, you're unlikely to win a dispute with them – they'll always try to protect their job and reputation.

That's why you need to negotiate directly with the project director as soon as possible. If you handled the kickoff meeting properly, the project director was likely present, and you'll also have regular check-in meetings.

This should give you a relationship with the project director, making it easier to speak with them directly. Don't get comfortable dealing only with the project manager. Go to the project director as soon as an issue arises.

Project directors have the authority to make decisions quickly, unlike their project managers. If you try to resolve conflicts only with the project manager, they'll likely delay in an effort to prevent them from looking bad.

Mistakes happen, and project managers often want to hide them. Identify who made the mistake and address it promptly.

Think about golf. It's a beautiful but frustrating game. You can still win as long as you get the ball in the hole, even if your swings aren't pretty. The guy with the big drive may look impressive, but you're focused on getting the ball in the hole in fewer strokes.

You understand the game – it's not about looking good, it's about finishing efficiently.

In disputes, it's the same. Both sides lose, so the goal is to lose the least. Get in front of the conflict early and avoid disputes whenever possible.

You might worry: *If I go over the project manager's head, won't that hurt my relationship with them?*

You should always try to resolve the issue with the project manager first. But if you're sure you're right and they're not listening, go to their project director.

The project manager might be taken aback, but they'll fall in line quickly once the project director is involved.

If the project manager is covering things up, escalate the issue. Explain your cashflow concerns and that despite your best efforts, the project manager isn't listening.

Since you already have a relationship with the project director, you can now work directly with them to resolve the problem. Always go to the person who can actually make decisions.

> **PRO TIP: MAKE THE PROJECT MANAGER LOOK GOOD**
>
> When you come across a conflict – not yet a dispute – ask yourself if you made a mistake. If you did, own it and try to resolve the issue with the project manager first.
>
> In a moment, I'll show you how to have this conversation in a way that makes it easier and smoother.
>
> If you can't resolve the issue and it's going to impact your cashflow, bring it up with the project director at your next check-in. If that's too far off, don't wait – pick up the phone and use the model I'll share shortly.
>
> In your conversation, aim to make the project manager look good.
>
> For example, say something like, 'John (The Project Manager) has been great to work with on this project, and we've been getting along well. We just have this one issue that's affecting our cashflow, and I'd like to get it resolved quickly so we can keep moving forward.'
>
> That's it. You might feel hesitant, especially if you've had this type of conversation go badly in the past.
>
> But don't worry – I'll walk you through it using the GROW Model.

Staying out of court

Let's assume you haven't been able to resolve a conflict, and now it's officially a dispute. Your main goal is to stay out of court, make a deal, and move on.

If the de-escalation talk did not resolve the conflict, the contract's dispute notice triggers the dispute process. Typically, a dispute notice triggers the next step, which is to go to court.

There are two things I don't like about this clause in most contracts. First, it doesn't allow a conversation with leadership.

Even if they want to discuss the issue, the contract forces them to follow the court process unless they make big moves. This puts you in a tricky spot.

You don't want to breach the contract, but their lawyers might advise going straight to court, which is bad news for you.

Secondly, going to court is expensive – easily hundreds of thousands of dollars. If your dispute is for $20,000, for example, it makes no sense to go to court, as the cost will outweigh the claim.

You need to negotiate a key step in the dispute clause. It should require you and their project director to meet before heading to court. Court is costly for both sides, and the only real winners are the lawyers.

Instead, you want to replace the court step with a cheaper, quicker option like mediation or adjudication.

Arbitration is not the answer either. Arbitration is essentially another version of going to court.

Don't confuse arbitration with adjudication. Adjudication is a quick, binding decision from an independent adjudicator, like a retired construction lawyer or business owner.

Mediation involves an independent person helping both sides talk through the dispute to find a solution. (These options may vary by location, depending on the local laws.)

In either case, you need to strike a deal. In any negotiation, you'll have to compromise. Do it early, and for as little as possible. This approach will save you money, resolve the issue faster, and protect your relationship with the client.

One business owner I worked with, who ran a mobile drilling company, found himself in a dispute. His client hadn't paid over $800,000 due to a disagreement over part of the invoice.

The owner was set on going to court, so I advised him to hire a lawyer. After his first consultation, the lawyer gave him an estimate: it would cost at least $200,000 to go to court, with no guarantee of winning.

The owner realised he was gambling $1,000,000 to win $600,000, which didn't make sense.

> $1,000,000 if he loses = $800k claim lost + $200k in lawyer's fees
>
> $600,000 if he wins = $800k claim won − $200k in lawyer's fees

So how could he have avoided this?

His client hadn't refused to pay the full $800,000 – they only disputed a small part of the invoice. If he had agreed to a 10% discount, he could've settled for $720,000 and moved on.

If you find yourself heading towards a dispute, the first thing you should do is file a dispute notice.

As the one most invested in resolving the issue, you'll likely be the one to initiate it. Send a formal letter to leadership, per the contract. Request a meeting to discuss the issue.

If that doesn't work, follow the contract's mediation or adjudication process. Be prepared with all the documentation, facts, and a clear understanding of your financial position.

> **PRO TIP: TAKE A REASONABLE DEAL**
>
> At any point, if you get the chance to make a deal that's reasonable, take it. Whether you propose, compromise, or accept, it's better to lose a little money upfront than to lose much more later.

The GROW Model

☺ → X → 🔄 → GROW

Let them speak — Don't interrupt — Give it back to them — Implement model

When it comes to disputes or disagreements, the GROW Model is a powerful tool. Originally developed by business coaches in the 1980s, I've adapted it specifically for construction industry conflicts.

Before diving into the construction GROW Model, there's one thing to keep in mind: in meetings like these, people often get bogged down in irrelevant details. It derails the conversation and distracts from the big issues.

The goal is to agree on a number and move on. No one wants to waste time discussing the specifics of what happened at a particular moment. Keep the conversation focused on the high-level matters.

Meetings can also get heated, with people talking over one another. To control this, make sure the other side feels heard. This method is simple but effective. You might be tired of their shouting, but hear me out – there's a reason behind it.

Start by saying: 'Look, we both have our opinions on what happened. I'd like to hear where you stand on this issue.'

Let them speak without interruption. As they talk, take notes.

When they finish, repeat their concerns back to them: 'What I'm hearing is X, Y, and Z. Did I get that right?'

You want them to confirm. Once they do, you move into the GROW Model.

The reason you didn't interrupt them is so that they can't interrupt you when it's your turn. You need to get through the GROW Model without being interrupted for it to be effective.

If they try, you can politely say: 'I didn't interrupt you – could you please give me the same courtesy' – they'll stop right away.

Now, here's the GROW Model:

- **G for Goal**

   Start by setting the goal: the goal is to maintain a good relationship, keep working on this project, and resolve this issue fairly.

   What you need to say here is, 'The goal is to continue to have a great relationship with you, work on the project, and get this resolved reasonably.'

- **R for Reality**

   This is where you present your side, using facts only. No emotions, just data, evidence, and the truth.

- **O for Options**

   Offer them two or three options:

   > Option 1: 'We can continue this dispute, get the lawyers involved, and go to court.'
   >
   > Option 2: Present the compromise you want, like offering to take 10% off the figure.
   >
   > Option 3: A bad option, such as stopping work, which would disrupt the project and your cashflow. This causes problems for everybody.

   The second option should be the one you want them to take. Always make your offer slightly below what you really want, so you have room to negotiate.

- **W for Way forward**

   Ask *them* to choose one of your options. If they pick the dispute route, you know where you stand. But most of the time, they'll want to settle and negotiate on the best option.

The GROW Model helps keep hot-headed conversations calm and focused on the bigger picture. It also puts you in control of the situation.

Many of our clients say it gives them confidence going into meetings because they know they'll come out with the best result. It organises how you handle the conversation, giving you control and helping you achieve a good outcome.

You might feel a bit strange the first time you follow a process like this, but it works. Hundreds of our clients use it successfully, and after a while it becomes second nature.

Remember the guy hacking the ball down the middle of the golf course? The goal isn't to have perfect shots – it's to get the ball in the hole with the fewest strokes. Which is to get a deal done and move on.

CHAPTER 7 ACTION ITEM: IDENTIFY AND ADDRESS POTENTIAL CONFLICTS EARLY

Step 1: Look over your current projects and identify any potential conflicts – whether it's a delayed payment, additional work not yet agreed upon, or miscommunication over responsibilities.

Step 2: Once identified, schedule a check-in with the project manager or client to address the issue before it escalates. Use the GROW Model to guide your conversation and steer it towards resolution.

Step 3: Make sure you document everything discussed and agreed upon to keep the situation clear and avoid future misunderstandings.

Why: Addressing potential conflicts early prevents them from escalating into costly disputes and protects your cashflow and relationships.

Chapter 8
From bidding wars to trusted partnerships

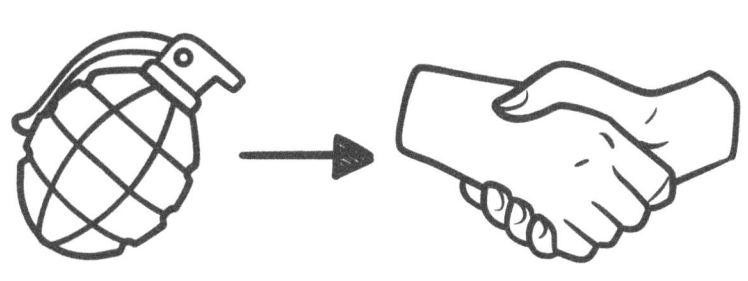

Chapter 8 summary

In this chapter, we dive into the critical process of turning short-term projects into long-term, profitable relationships.

By following a clear, proven process for conducting client check-ins and 'upselling' before a project ends, you can lock in framework agreements that create a stable pipeline of work.

This approach not only removes the awkwardness often associated with pursuing more work but also positions you as a trusted partner rather than just another bidder.

Highlights

- Why setting up regular check-in meetings is the key to long-term client relationships.
- How to use the check-in process to improve your work and strengthen your client's trust.
- The perfect moment to upsell to a framework agreement.
- How to manage the framework agreement process, including timelines, follow-ups, and navigating potential delays.
- Why consistency theory makes it easier to get clients to commit.

'The best way to predict the future is to create it.'

Peter Drucker

How to stop chasing projects and start building relationships that last

You need a process to build long-term relationships with clients who have consistent work – this helps you move away from constantly bidding on jobs. By doing so, you'll avoid the extreme highs and lows typical of the construction industry.

It's important to say that 'black swan events' such as COVID and the Global Financial Crisis will continue to occur over your lifetime and construction as a whole will be impacted. In those scenarios, when the whole market is suffering and risk is at an all-time high, who do you think clients are going to award work to?

- Someone they have never worked with?
- Someone they trust and already have a framework agreement with?

In our kickoff meeting chapter, we discussed starting your sales process by taking control and scheduling four check-in meetings.

The first and second check-ins are very similar but still crucial. The third check-in is where the magic happens – this is when you transition the client into a long-term relationship by getting them to agree to a framework agreement.

> **QUICK REMINDER: FRAMEWORK AGREEMENTS**
>
> A framework agreement is a long-term deal between two parties that sets basic terms for future work.
>
> It makes it easy to issue contracts, often called 'call-offs', so the subcontractor can start work without needing long contract negotiations every time.
>
> Getting a framework agreement in place is crucial for both sides because it simplifies the process and saves time.
>
> **For the client:** A framework agreement speeds up the process. Instead of negotiating new contracts for every project, they can issue a call-off, and work begins right away.
>
> There is less internal friction and fewer approvals for the main contractor.
>
> Having trusted subcontractors ready to go ensures projects move quickly, and agreeing on terms upfront avoids future disputes.
>
> **For the subcontractor (you):** A framework agreement provides security. You don't have to constantly bid for new work.
>
> It turns you from just another bidder into a trusted partner. This gives you stability, repeat business, and better resource planning. Plus, you avoid the risk of last-minute changes or unfavourable terms when things are rushed.
>
> Getting a framework agreement done benefits both sides by reducing delays, minimising disputes, and ensuring steady work with less hassle.

The fourth check-in is essentially a final reminder to get the framework agreement signed.

This is your last chance to secure it before the project ends. Once the project wraps up and people move on, it becomes much harder to lock in the agreement.

The goal here is to shift away from relying solely on competitive bidding to secure work. You still start with bidding but aim to transition into long-term partnerships.

Ideally, you'll reach a point where you have enough steady relationships that competitive bidding becomes unnecessary.

Creating long-term relationships

Everyone wants long-term relationships, but few discuss how to create them.

Choreographing the process is the most important part. Most subcontractors do good work, but when it comes time to secure future work, they fumble.

It gets awkward, and they waste the effort they've put in because the process feels uncomfortable. But when you follow a proven process, it becomes easy.

Clients feel confident that you're professional and reliable, which makes it easier for them to keep you on their books.

If you've delivered well in the past, they can trust you and will be happy to award work to someone with a good reputation.

Larger companies are proud of the quality of their supply chain, and you want to become one of their trusted subcontractors.

Think of it like assembling a complex piece of furniture from IKEA without the instructions. You might know the end goal, but without a clear process, you'll risk missing key steps. Following a process ensures everything works smoothly. Without one, you're guessing.

There are four meetings, which we outlined in chapter 5. This chapter explains what happens during each meeting and provides scripts for the upsell and final meetings.

Following this structure will help you avoid the awkwardness you may have experienced in the past. The result is a framework agreement that supports your long-term relationship with the client.

Timing of the upsell

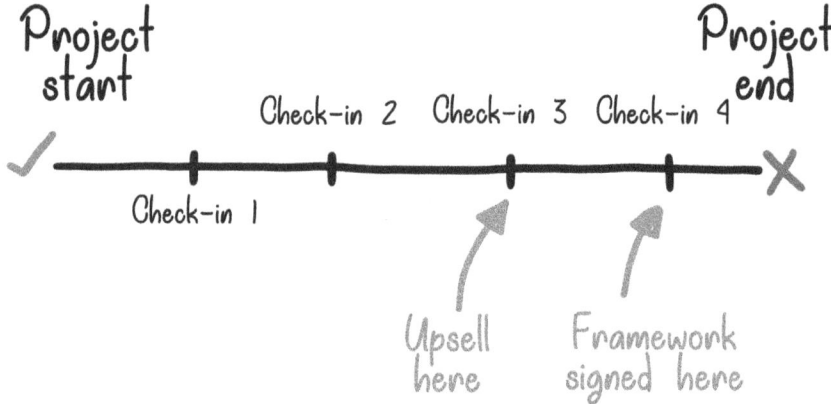

The upsell should happen 75% of the way through the project, not at the end. Most subcontractors try to upsell when the project is finished, or nearly so.

The problem with that approach is you've run out of time. You can't follow up or discuss details with their internal team because they've already shifted focus to other projects. You're out of sight and out of mind.

By doing the upsell at 75% project completion (or in the third check-in meeting), you leave enough time to discuss details with their contract team and to follow up. You'll even have one more meeting to finalise things before the project ends.

If you wait until the project is over, your chances of getting the framework agreement signed drop significantly.

By staying visible and keeping the conversation going, you're more likely to get the agreement signed and secure the relationship.

People work with people, not businesses.

Our most successful clients have a small group of clients with whom they have excellent working relationships which continue to grow and develop. There is no deception, no bullshit, no back-stabbing. The rules are clear but most importantly the people work with each other.

One of our clients, IPTel, who has been implementing this process, has managed to secure three Master Service Agreements in six months, each with a different company they work well with, for a period of three years.

Imagine what it does to your business to be able to forecast what work you have coming up in the next three years and what the terms of the contract are going to be.

Game changer.

Think about your own business. Have you ever had a supplier or vendor finish a project and send you an email asking if you'd be open to future work?

They don't call, or if they do, it feels desperate and awkward. The same thing happens if you wait too long to upsell – you lose momentum, and the client has moved on to other priorities.

You might be wondering: *How can we prove we've done a good job if we haven't finished the project yet?*

In check-ins one and two, you take control of the client's perception of your work by asking them what quality means to them – and then delivering it. By the time the upsell comes around, the quality of your work should be undeniable.

Follow the process and use the exact wording I'll give you. If you're worried that the script doesn't sound like you, don't stress – clients can't tell, and you'll get used to it.

This is a proven method, and while you can personalise it, the content itself works as written.

Check-ins one and two

The first two check-ins are all about understanding what the client considers a good job and working together to achieve it.

These meetings follow a simple three-step process to ensure you're always aligned with their expectations.

Here's the three-step check-in process:

1. **Purpose:** Start by reminding the client why you're having this meeting.

For example, you could say: 'We're here to ensure we're doing a great job for you, but we need your feedback to make sure we're on the right track. How does that sound?'

2. **What's going well:** Ask the client what they think is going well. Then share your perspective – highlight what's working from your side too. This sets a positive tone and reinforces the good work already being done.

3. **What needs improvement:** Ask the client where they see room for improvement.

   Get them to focus on one specific area that you can work on. This keeps the feedback actionable and manageable.

In the first meeting, go through these three steps. Take note of what they want you to improve and make that your top priority. Build a plan around it, and ensure you deliver improvements by the next check-in.

In the second check-in, start by reminding the client of the one thing they asked you to improve. Then show them how you've addressed it – whether through data, a presentation, or clear examples.

After that, go through the three-step process again to see if there's another area where you can improve.

By the end of this check-in, you should have demonstrated that you can act on feedback and deliver high-quality results that are specific to what they consider to be 'valuable'.

It's important to remember that clients may have multiple subcontractors on-site, and they may not always know how well you're performing. These meetings help make sure your work is seen and appreciated, turning it into a collaborative effort.

Check-in three: the upsell

The third check-in is where you aim to get their commitment to sign a framework agreement, but you should still refer to it as a check-in to the client.

By now, you've done a lot of good work, but they might not always notice. This meeting is your chance to show them everything you've done, including any extra effort or favours.

Start by listing all the good work you've completed, even if it's not something you typically talk about.

For example, you can say: 'We did this for you, and we handled that issue for you.'

Then remind them of the improvements they requested in previous check-ins and show how you delivered on each of them. This reinforces that you can take feedback and consistently improve, and you could be a great long-term partner.

At this stage, the value you have provided should be undeniable. You have literally spelled it out for them.

The transition to discussing a framework agreement

To smoothly transition into the framework agreement discussion, use a casual approach.

First, ask them: 'Do you think we've done a good job for you so far?'

Then remind them of your initial conversation in the kickoff meeting: 'Do you remember in our kickoff meeting, you said that if we did a good job for you, you would be open to agreeing to a framework agreement with us? I think we can both agree that we've done a good job so far and we'd love to have a long-term relationship with you. Would you be opposed to starting that framework agreement process assuming we continue to deliver?'

Once they agree, ask if the framework agreement can be finalised at the next check-in.

You can say: 'Once the project ends it could be a bit harder with communication. We've already scheduled another check-in on [INSERT DATE]. Would it be fair enough to try to wrap up the framework agreement at that time?'

Why this matters

It can take months to negotiate a framework agreement due to bureaucracy, so getting their agreement early is essential.

Framework agreements can be complex and long, so starting now ensures you have enough time to finalise the details before the project ends. This keeps both parties aligned and avoids rushing through important discussions at the last minute.

Make connections and maintain them early on, so when it comes to the crunch you have representatives from your client in your corner to vouch for you.

It is business, but people work with people. Be a person people want to work with.

Yes, it is a corporate decision but if you can have the client's project director on your team it is much smoother sailing.

By running a structured process, delivering consistent value, and reminding them of the initial commitment, you increase your chances of securing a long-term partnership while avoiding awkward, last-minute negotiations.

Dealing with changes in commitment

What happens if they've changed their mind about the framework agreement since the start of the project?

This is unlikely, thanks to a concept called **consistency theory**, coined by Robert Cialdini in his book *Influence*.

The theory is based on the idea that people tend to act in ways that align with their past commitments and beliefs. Once someone makes a decision, they are more likely to follow through to stay consistent with their initial commitment.

If your client agreed to consider a framework agreement earlier in the project (at the kickoff meeting), they're more likely to continue down that path. Even small agreements can lead to bigger decisions later.

However, if something has changed and they've shifted their stance on the agreement, you'll know early enough to adjust.

You've still delivered a solid process by asking what they value, improving based on their feedback, and showing your ability to meet their needs. This will positively impact your reputation, and maintaining consistency is far more likely than an unexpected change.

The fortune is in the follow-up

Learn the scripts and practise them until they feel natural. You can tweak the wording to suit your style, but stick to the script's intent.

If you're unsure, don't change anything – each word is carefully chosen to come across naturally. If you struggle to make the script feel natural, ask yourself: *Do you want a stable business, or are you more concerned with how the words sound?*

Priorities matter.

A key principle of successful sales is that **'the fortune is in the follow-up'.**

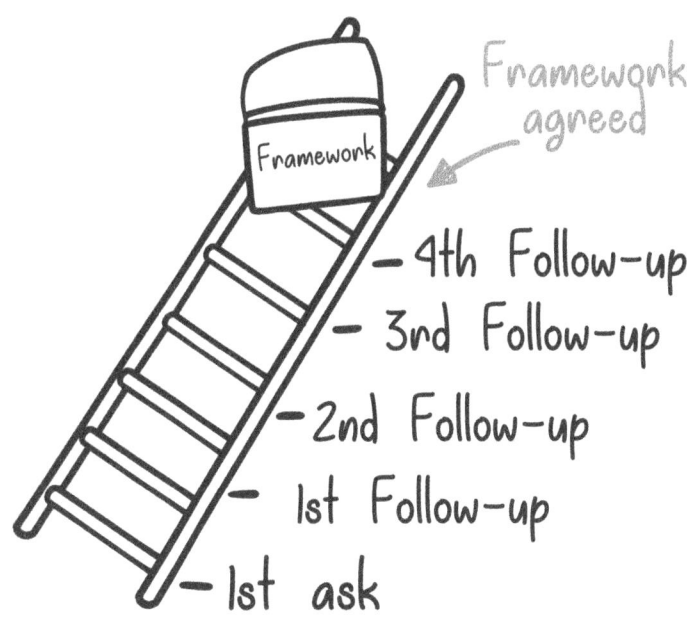

Just because you have a verbal agreement for a framework agreement doesn't mean the deal is done. You still need to push it across the finish line.

Until it's signed, you're still competing in the bidding process. To move forward, you need to know what the next steps are, who is responsible, and when it all needs to happen.

Treat this process like managing a construction project. Assign dates to each step. You're leading every meeting. Typically, you'll need to connect with their lawyer, commercial manager, or contracts manager.

Once you've made that introduction, they'll send over the contract for negotiation. From there, negotiate as outlined in chapter 4, then finalise the agreement.

> **KEY POINT: DRIVE THE PROCESS**
>
> Keep in mind, getting the framework agreement done is **your** priority, not theirs. It's important to them, but it won't feel urgent.
>
> It's up to you to drive the process forward, as they're likely to get bogged down in bureaucracy.

Here's an example from a typical construction scenario.

Subcontractors hired for a large project had just completed the design and scope for electrical services. But before ordering materials and mobilising the crew, they needed the main contractor's approval.

Delays in approval would mess up their cashflow and project schedule, so the subcontractors submitted their final design and pricing.

They assumed the main contractor would quickly review and approve it. Days passed, but nothing happened.

The subcontractors felt the pressure mounting. Any further delay would push back procurement and ripple through their entire schedule. They had other jobs lined up, and if this one stalled, it would turn into a scheduling disaster.

For the main contractor, however, electrical work wasn't a top priority at the moment. Other trades were working, and their focus was on meeting deadlines for structural elements. To them, the subcontractor's work could wait.

Recognising the urgency, the subcontractor started following up regularly – sending reminder emails and requesting meetings to keep the approval process moving.

Eventually, the main contractor acknowledged the delay, signed off on the design, and the subcontractor was able to order materials and keep the schedule on track.

If they hadn't followed up, they'd have faced costly delays, lost revenue, and potential reputational damage.

In this situation, the subcontractor's persistence made all the difference. The main contractor had other priorities, but the urgency was on the subcontractor's side. Their follow-up kept the project moving and protected their business.

In the same way, it's your responsibility to get the framework agreement over the line. If you're worried about coming across as pushy, don't be.

People get busy and forget, but they often appreciate the reminder. They'll also be grateful that you're leading this stage. Find out the next steps, assign dates, and keep moving forward.

Check-in four: finalising the framework agreement

If the process does stall, the final check-in is your opportunity to reignite momentum and get everything back on track.

This meeting is designed to push through any last-minute hesitations, address any remaining concerns, and ensure the framework agreement is finalised.

While it's rare for things to stall, this check-in acts as your safety net – one final push to secure the deal.

Remember, at this stage you're not introducing new information or starting fresh negotiations. You're simply reinforcing the commitment the client has already made.

Use this check-in to remind them of the value you've provided throughout the project, and why moving forward with a framework agreement benefits both sides.

Here are a few key steps to follow in this final check-in:

1. **Reinforce the relationship:** Remind the client of the successful collaboration you've had.

    Highlight the key wins from the project and the improvements you made based on their feedback. By now, they've seen your ability to deliver and adapt – this is your chance to reinforce the trust you've built.

2. **Frame the framework agreement as a win–win:** Emphasise how the framework agreement will streamline future projects and eliminate the need for repeated negotiations.

Let them know that this is a time-saving tool that will benefit both parties and ensure smoother, faster engagements moving forward.

3. **Push for finalisation:** Politely but firmly, push for the framework agreement to be signed before the project ends.

   You can say something like: 'I'd love to get the framework in place before we wrap up, while everything is fresh and we've got great momentum. It'll save us both time and ensure we're ready for any future work.'

Lastly, **always remember BAMFAM** – 'book a meeting from a meeting'. Before you leave the check-in, lock in a date for when the agreement will be finalised.

Even if things are moving smoothly, this strategy ensures there's always forward momentum, preventing any unnecessary delays. You don't want to be chasing signatures after the project ends when communication becomes more difficult.

By running a structured process, staying proactive, and keeping the client engaged, you greatly increase your chances of finalising the framework agreement and setting the stage for a long-term partnership.

Successful subcontractors agree frameworks all the time. Why can't you too?

CHAPTER 8 ACTION ITEM: START SCHEDULING YOUR CHECK-IN MEETINGS NOW

Step 1: Identify one or two of your current or upcoming projects.

Step 2: Schedule four check-in meetings with your client, spreading them throughout the project's timeline. Make sure to include a meeting at 75% project completion.

Step 3: Prepare a simple agenda for each meeting, focusing on client feedback and demonstrating your progress. Use this opportunity to guide the conversation toward securing a framework agreement before the project ends.

Why: Setting up these check-ins ensures you stay top-of-mind for your client, giving you the chance to upsell before the project is over, and helping you transition into a long-term partnership without relying on constant bidding.

Chapter 9
The road map

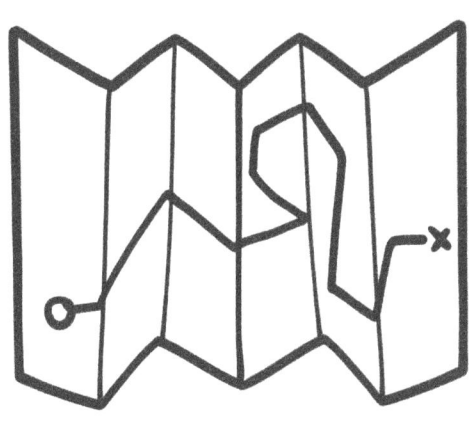

Chapter 9 summary

This final chapter consolidates everything you've learned throughout the book into one actionable roadmap, guiding you step by step to transform your construction business.

If you're dealing with cashflow problems, stuck in low-margin bidding, or trying to stabilise your business and build lasting relationships, this chapter gives you practical steps to overcome these challenges.

The road map

> 'The secret of change is to focus all of your energy, not on fighting the old, but on building the new.'
>
> Socrates

Before you started reading this book, you might have been feeling the pressure.

Always stressed about paying your team on time, watching your margins shrink with every project. No matter how hard you worked, the cashflow never seemed to give you a break.

You were stuck, moving from project to project with no real stability, no long-term clients, and no certainty about what was coming next.

Each job felt like a battle – bidding lower just to win, competing against subcontractors who slashed their prices even further. When the job ended, there was no celebration, only the anxiety of wondering if the payment would arrive in time to keep the business afloat.

It was frustrating, exhausting, and despite all the hard work, it felt like you were just spinning your wheels, trapped in the same cycle, waiting for things to finally get easier.

But now, things are different. You've made it through this book, and you have the tools to break free from the bidding wars, the cashflow struggles, and the endless short-term projects.

In this chapter, we're going to bring everything together into one clear, actionable roadmap.

This is your step-by-step guide to building a business that's stable, growing, and built for long-term success – no matter where you are right now.

Phase 1: Secure upfront payments on new projects

Cashflow issues are the number one reason subcontractors struggle. One of the quickest ways to fix this is by securing upfront payments.

You need to break free from the deferred payment model, where you're waiting 30, 60, or even 90 days to get paid for work you've already done. Instead, aim for a prepaid payment model, where you get paid upfront for your services.

This can be done by submitting alternative bids that give the client a discount in exchange for prepayment.

It's a win–win: clients love discounts, and you get the cash you need to start the project strong, and you can make up your margins with a strong change and delay system (phase 3).

Remember this is to get your foot in the door to turn these clients into a long-term relationship.

This simple shift in how you structure your payment terms will make a huge difference in your cashflow and allow you to better manage your business.

Action: Start proposing upfront payments as standard, and if it's not possible, try submitting alternative bids that offer a discount for prepayment.

Use this strategy to get cash flowing upfront and remove the stress of waiting for payments.

Phase 2: Negotiate better contract terms

'The returns are in the terms.'

The purpose of negotiating better contract terms is not just to increase margins but also to reduce risk and protect your business.

Over a 10-year span, something will inevitably go wrong – whether it's delays, unforeseen scope changes, or other project disruptions.

The question isn't if, but when. And when it does happen, you want it to be a minor inconvenience, not a disaster that threatens your company.

Negotiating better contract terms is vital to protecting your business. It's about putting safeguards in place that allow you to get paid fairly, with the right party accepting the appropriate risk, and giving you the leverage to get changes and delays approved when they arise.

Without strong terms, you're exposed to greater risk and losing potential profit or even your entire company.

This isn't optional. It's a critical part of running a sustainable, profitable business. The terms you negotiate today will protect your margins and cashflow tomorrow, ensuring that your projects run smoothly and setbacks don't cause financial strain.

Action: You need to make this a priority. Learn how to negotiate better contracts yourself, hire someone internally who understands how to protect your interests, or seek external expertise.

Whatever you choose, you must have a system in place to make sure you're negotiating the best possible terms – *this is non-negotiable if you want to succeed.*

Phase 3: Implement a system for changes and delays

This is where all the money is made.

The margin and cashflow that can make or break a project are often hidden in how changes and delays are handled. Without a system in place to address variations and delays as they occur, you're leaving significant profit on the table and exposing yourself to unnecessary risk.

You need a clear, structured process for identifying, documenting, submitting, and getting approvals for changes and delays.

This process must be fast and efficient. Every delay or change that goes unaccounted for is money lost, and without a system, chaos can quickly ensue.

When managed correctly, however, these changes can actually increase your margins and provide a buffer for your cashflow.

This step is absolutely essential. The margin and cashflow are in the post-award process, and without a system, you're simply not maximising the potential of your projects.

If you don't actively manage changes and delays, you're not just losing profit – you're putting your entire project at risk.

Action: You must have this system in place. Either train someone internally who understands how to manage changes and delays effectively, or bring in external support to handle it for you.

This is not a step you can afford to skip. It's crucial to maintaining profitability and ensuring your business can thrive.

Phase 4: The kickoff meeting – your secret weapon

Once the contract is signed, the kickoff meeting is your opportunity to take control of the project. This isn't just about introducing the team – it's about establishing your authority, setting expectations, and laying the foundation for a long-term relationship.

Your secret weapon lies in ensuring this meeting is led by you, where you set the agenda and goals for the entire project.

This is also where you schedule your four check-ins. Your new sales process.

These will be crucial for managing the client relationship, making sure you stay on top of any potential issues, and positioning yourself for the upsell to a framework agreement later.

Key actions:

- Lead the kickoff meeting. Set the agenda, clarify goals, and establish yourself as the authority.
- Schedule your four check-ins during the kickoff meeting, ensuring you stay in control of the client relationship.

Phase 5: Master the check-ins and the upsell

Your check-ins are the backbone of the client relationship and the path to long-term partnerships.

The purpose is to show your value, gather feedback, and implement improvements. By doing this regularly, you're proving that you can deliver, and you're building trust.

By following this process, you make your value undeniable.

The critical moment happens in the third check-in, which takes place at around 75% of project completion.

This is where you introduce the upsell – your opportunity to transition the client from a one-off project to a long-term relationship through a framework agreement.

Remember, this isn't just another meeting – it's a pivotal moment to move away from competitive bidding and secure repeat business.

You need to master the scripts, the timing, and the process.

The fortune is in the follow-up, and the success of this step will determine whether you stay in the low-margin world of bidding or move into profitable, long-term relationships.

Key actions:

- Use check-ins 1 and 2 to demonstrate your value.
- At the third check-in, upsell the framework agreement and make sure it's signed by the fourth check-in.

Phase 6: Build your premium brand

At this point, you're establishing a more stable business, but you're not done yet. Now is the time to elevate your company's reputation and build a premium brand.

This phase is about marketing yourself as the top choice in the industry – not the cheapest, but the best.

To do this, you need to prove your value. One of the most effective ways to build credibility is through testimonials.

After every project, you should be collecting feedback and turning that into social proof. Build a system where testimonials are gathered automatically and used across your website, proposals, and marketing materials.

This isn't about price anymore – it's about positioning your business as a premium provider that delivers high-quality, reliable work.

This phase is crucial to moving away from low-margin jobs and ensuring you get the clients and projects you want.

Key actions:

- Develop a system for collecting testimonials after every project.
- Use those testimonials to market yourself as a premium brand, focusing on quality and reliability.

Phase 7: Master dispute avoidance

Disputes are an inevitable part of any construction project. Despite the best efforts to plan, negotiate better contracts, and manage changes effectively, there will be times when disagreements arise.

The key to managing disputes is to handle them quickly and efficiently, ensuring they don't escalate into something larger that threatens the project's completion, your reputation, or your relationship with the client.

When it comes to disputes, speed and clarity are essential. This phase focuses on developing a clear, systematic approach to handling disagreements, whether they involve delays, scope changes, or payment issues.

Your goal in this phase is to resolve disputes early through clear communication, documented processes, and, if necessary, formal dispute resolution mechanisms such as mediation or adjudication (depending on your country).

Key actions:

- *Maintain strong documentation:* Document every communication, change, and variation as it happens. This documentation will be vital if a dispute arises, and in most cases reduces the chances of disputes entirely.

- *Use the GROW Model:* Aim to resolve disputes informally through negotiation before they become formal claims. Use the GROW Model to achieve an outcome quickly.

Phase 8: Transition to framework agreements and cultivate relationships

Repeat phases 1 through 7 with each new client until you have many framework agreements.

Now, you have developed a strong, relationship-based list of clients who are happy to pay a little extra because they know you can deliver.

It is also much easier for them internally to engage you, so you should get additional work.

This is where your business moves from chasing projects to having a steady pipeline of repeat work with key clients.

A framework agreement locks in long-term relationships, giving you the security of ongoing projects without having to constantly bid for new work.

The real money in this business is made in relationships, and that's why cultivating them is your next priority.

Even when you're not actively working on a project, you should remain in contact with your clients, offering value and staying top-of-mind. This ensures that when they have more work, you're their go-to subcontractor.

This final step is about locking in stability. You've worked hard to get to this point, and now it's about making sure you maintain those relationships and grow them over time. Consistency is key.

Key actions:

- Repeat phases 1 to 7 until you have enough work through framework agreements alone.
- Continue to nurture those relationships, staying in regular contact and offering value even when you're not actively working.

Implementing this roadmap

By following this process, your business will transform in ways you may not have imagined.

Picture having steady work with predictable margins, knowing your team is not just busy today but for months or even years ahead.

Your clients won't see you as just another subcontractor – they'll view you as a trusted partner, the first one they call because they know you deliver.

You'll move away from the constant grind of chasing jobs and enjoy the freedom to focus on growth.

The frantic calls from the bank or suppliers will become a distant memory. Instead, your phone will ring with clients asking for your expertise, ready to commit to long-term relationships because they trust your ability to get the job done right.

Imagine the pride in seeing your business not just survive but thrive. You'll move from project to project with confidence, and your competitors will wonder how you're securing so much work when they are struggling.

You won't be scrambling to keep the lights on anymore; you'll be running a smooth, well-oiled operation, with a team and reputation that commands respect.

With this roadmap, you'll gain the stability and peace of mind you've been working for.

What's next?

If you've made it this far, congratulations.

You are among the top 10% of people in the world who finish books. Almost there …

You've taken a huge step in gaining control of your construction business and moving towards the success you've been working so hard to achieve.

At this point, you've probably realised the importance of each phase outlined in the previous chapter.

Where are you now?

Now, you're likely in one of three positions.

Position 1: Ready to implement right now

You're excited to get started. You know that the strategies in this book are exactly what you need to break free from low-margin projects and start building lasting relationships.

You're eager to put these processes into place because you see the potential they hold for your business.

If that's where you are, fantastic! You're already ahead of most of your competition by simply recognising the value of proactive change. Now, it's time to get to work.

Take it step by step. The journey towards a stronger, more profitable business begins now.

Position 2: Feeling overwhelmed by the volume of information

If you're feeling overwhelmed by the sheer amount of information, that's okay too.

When you're presented with a lot of options, it's natural to feel anxious or uncertain about where to start. The good news is, you don't have to implement everything at once.

Pick one thing. Focus on the phase or action that seems the most manageable right now and take small steps towards implementing it.

As you gain momentum, it will get easier. Remember, change doesn't happen overnight, but consistent progress will lead to long-term success.

Position 3: Realising you need help

You've read the book and recognise that while the strategies make sense, you don't want to handle it all yourself. That's perfectly fine. Not every business owner has the time, resources, or desire to implement these changes alone.

If this sounds like you, it may be time to consider bringing in outside help. Whether you need someone to manage your contracts, streamline your processes, or build a system for changes and delays, finding the right expertise can accelerate your progress.

At Quantum, we help subcontractors navigate these exact challenges every day. If you'd like to explore how we can work together, visit quantumcontracts.com and book a call with our team.

Final thoughts

Writing this book was a labour of love, driven by my deep belief that construction subcontractors deserve better. You deserve to run a business that not only survives but thrives, a business that brings you peace of mind, stability, and the respect you've earned through hard work.

The construction industry can be brutal – one wrong move and your entire livelihood can be at risk. But it's you who takes these risks so we can build our future and for that, I thank you.

I hope that one day your grandkids will drive by something you built and shout, 'My granddad built that!'

The future of your business is in your hands. Now, it's time to take action and build something great.

Could I please ask you a favour? Please share this with other construction people by leaving a review. It would mean the absolute world to me.

Bonus chapter

Commercial principles

> 'Success is where preparation and opportunity meet.'
>
> Bobby Unser

Contract sections for ~~dummies~~ legends

Most subcontractors know contracts matter, but few know the full impact of each section.

To make understanding these details easier, this bonus chapter breaks down the essentials of contract negotiation into simple language. You'll find plain explanations for each section, why it's critical to your bottom line, and tips for negotiating favourable terms.

Please note that these definitions are not all-encompassing. They are very high-level and designed to give you an idea, not an in-depth understanding.

Money makers

1. PAYMENT TERMS

What this means

When and often overlooked the process for getting paid.

Type of company this is important for

All companies.

Why it's important to negotiate this

Negotiating shorter payment terms – like 30 days instead of 60 – gives you faster access to cash, reducing reliance on credit or loans and helping you cover expenses like payroll and supplier payments.

But payment terms are only part of the picture. The entire payment process matters too.

In some contracts there is a requirement to submit a payment application first. Then, the client reviews and approves it – a process that can take time. Only after approval can you issue an invoice, and that is when the agreed payment terms (for example, 30 days) start.

When negotiating, you are not just asking for shorter terms like '30 days'. You are aiming to reduce the whole payment cycle – from submitting your payment application to getting paid – so cash reaches your account as quickly as possible.

2. INTEREST ON LATE PAYMENTS

What this means

Pretty straightforward. Your client pays you interest on their late payments at an agreed amount that is specified in the contract.

Type of company this is important for

All companies.

Why it's important to negotiate this

In my entire career, I have never seen this enforced. So then, why bother?

1. It serves as a tool that you can use. If you haven't been paid, hurry them up.
2. You can add it to a claim, and you are then willing to remove it as part of your negotiation.

3. EXTENSION OF TIME (EOT) CLAIM

What this means

A claim to extend the delivery date of your project, often with associated costs for that delay. (Costs are discussed in the next section.)

Type of company this is important for

All companies.

Why it's important to negotiate this

Without an EOT clause, you're at risk of penalties like liquidated damages for delays outside your control. For example, if heavy rainfall halts your excavation work for a week, an EOT clause allows you to adjust the timeline without penalty. This protects your profit margins and ensures you're not unfairly held responsible for uncontrollable events.

4. DELAY COSTS

What this means

Are you going to get paid or not for a delay. If so, how much?

Type of company this is important for

All companies.

Why it's important to negotiate this

Including a delay cost provision allows you to recover expenses when delays occur through no fault of your own. For example, if a client fails to provide necessary approvals on time, you can claim costs for idle labour and equipment.

5. CHANGE ORDERS/VARIATIONS

What this means

A change order/variation clause outlines the process for handling client-requested modifications after the project has started. It ensures any adjustments are documented, fairly priced, and agreed upon before work begins.

Type of company this is important for

All construction companies, especially those in trades like civil, structural, mechanical, and electrical work, where scope changes are common.

Why it's important to negotiate this

Without a change order process, you might end up absorbing the costs of additional work. By negotiating this, you ensure you're compensated for any extra labour, materials, or overheads resulting from client-initiated changes, protecting your profit margins.

6. RISE AND FALL OR ESCALATION

What this means

A rise and fall (or escalation) clause allows for contract price adjustments if material costs increase significantly during the project.

Type of company this is important for

Companies dependent on materials with volatile prices – such as steel fabricators, concrete suppliers, and rebar manufacturers.

Why it's important to negotiate this

Including an escalation clause prepares you for market changes. For instance, if steel prices surge by 20% mid-project, just like during COVID.

7. UNFIXED PLANT AND MATERIALS

What this means

An unfixed plant and materials clause allows you to claim payment for materials as soon as they are delivered or stored off-site, even before they're installed.

Type of company this is important for

Contractors with significant material costs – like those in steel fabrication, electrical, or mechanical industries.

Why it's important to negotiate this

What can happen here is that you may have agreed to be paid when your materials are installed. There may be a delay to the installation that is not your fault and you will not be paid, leaving you to absorb the costs.

Company enders

1. LIMITATION OF LIABILITY

What this means

A limitation of liability clause sets a cap on the amount you're responsible for if something goes wrong.

Type of company this is important for

All construction companies, especially those involved in large projects where potential risks and liabilities are higher.

Why it's important to negotiate this

By capping your liability – say, at 100% of the contract value – you know your maximum financial exposure upfront. This clarity allows you to focus on delivering quality work without fear of overwhelming risks.

2. CONSEQUENTIAL DAMAGE OR LOSS

What this means

Essentially – your client's loss of profit for something you did.

Type of company this is important for

All contractors, particularly in civil, structural, or mechanical construction, where projects involve complex, interconnected tasks.

Why it's important to negotiate this

Your client's loss of profit could be the entire size of your company.

3. INDEMNIFICATION

What this means

Who's responsible to cover specific damages like property damage or injury resulting from your work?

Type of company this is important for

Contractors overseeing projects with multiple parties on-site, such as general contractors and those in civil or mechanical fields.

Why it's important to negotiate this

A well-defined indemnity clause limits your liability to damages caused by your own work. By keeping indemnities specific and reciprocal – where each party covers its own risks – you avoid unexpected liabilities and financial traps.

4. LIQUIDATED DAMAGES (LDS)

What this means

Liquidated damages are a pre-agreed cost per a certain period (usually per day or week) of time that you have to pay the client if you are late.

Type of company this is important for

All contractors, especially those managing large projects with tight deadlines.

Why it's important to negotiate this

Sometimes they are extortionate and the costs have no basis in reality. You can negotiate this down to something reasonable so if they were to occur the impact is not so severe.

5. TERMINATION

What this means

This outlines the steps if either party fails to meet their obligations.

Type of company this is important for

Contractors involved in high-investment or long-term projects, such as commercial construction and infrastructure development.

Why it's important to negotiate this

Many times the client will list all the ways in which they can terminate you if you have not met your obligations and be silent on what happens if they don't meet their obligations. For example, if they don't pay you on time.

6. SECURITY

What this means

Security clauses involve holding back a percentage of the contract value as assurance for project completion. This can be done either by retention (the physical hold back of money on each invoice), bank guarantee, or insurance bond.

Type of company this is important for

Most construction companies working on larger projects, except those providing temporary works like scaffolding or traffic management.

Why it's important to negotiate this

Negotiating a fair structure for security release – such as releasing half upon project completion and the rest after the defects liability period (explained in the next section) – ensures you have access to funds when needed, supporting steady cashflow.

7. DEFECTS LIABILITY PERIOD (DLP)

What this means

The DLP is a set period after project completion during which you're responsible for fixing any issues within your scope of work. An overly long DLP can tie up resources that could be spent on new projects.

Type of company this is important for

All construction companies, especially those in civil, structural, and mechanical sectors where clients expect lasting quality.

Why it's important to negotiate this

Setting a reasonable DLP – typically 12 months – balances client assurance with your need to move on to new projects. It ensures you're not indefinitely responsible for maintenance beyond the project's reasonable timeframe.

8. DEED OF GUARANTEE

What this means

This is essentially you personally guaranteeing the success of the project.

Type of company this is important for

Companies in civil, structural, or mechanical construction where projects require substantial capital and clients seek additional assurances.

Why it's important to negotiate this

This is just a no-no. The risk is not worth the reward.

9. PROPORTIONATE LIABILITY

What this means

A proportionate liability clause limits your responsibility to the specific work you've handled. In case of a problem, you're only liable for your part, not the entire project.

Type of company this is important for

Contractors on large, multi-contractor projects – like electrical, civil, and mechanical contractors – where many teams contribute to the outcome.

Why it's important to negotiate this

This clause ensures that liability is shared fairly among all parties based on their level of responsibility. It prevents you from bearing the financial impact of others' mistakes, keeping your liability focused on your work alone.

Paperwork streamliners

1. HEAD CONTRACT/PRIME CONTRACT PROVISIONS

What this means

A head contract or prime contract is the main agreement between the project owner and the principal contractor. Sometimes, terms from this contract can 'flow down' to subcontractors, making them responsible for obligations they didn't directly agree to.

Who this is important for

Contractors working on large projects with multiple subcontractors and stakeholders need to understand how head contract clauses affect them.

Why it's important to negotiate this

By reviewing and negotiating your subcontract, you can prevent unintended obligations from the head contract flowing down to you. This ensures you're only responsible for risks you've explicitly agreed to, protecting your business from unexpected liabilities.

2. DISPUTE RESOLUTION

What this means

A dispute resolution clause outlines the steps for resolving conflicts.

Type of company this is important for

All companies.

Why it's important to negotiate this

We need a structure that actually works in your favour to resolve the dispute. We talked about this is detail in the dispute chapter.

3. NOTIFICATION PERIODS

What this means

Notification periods specify how quickly you need to inform the client when requesting things like extra time or changes in scope. Missing these deadlines can forfeit your rights.

Type of company this is important for

Contractors in fast-paced projects, particularly in construction, mechanical work, and civil engineering, where delays and changes are common.

Why it's important to negotiate this

Negotiating reasonable notification periods – like seven calendar days – ensures you have enough time to act. This protects you from losing the right to claim extensions or additional costs due to tight deadlines.

4. ASSESSMENT PERIODS

What this means

Assessment periods define how quickly the client must review and respond to your claims. This prevents delays and keeps the project moving forward.

Type of company this is important for

All contractors, especially those whose progress depends on timely client decisions, like those in construction, mechanical, and civil engineering.

Why it's important to negotiate this

Sometimes, clients take a long time to approve your claims, which can impact your cashflow. A defined assessment period ensures the client responds promptly and keeps things moving.

5. RISK AND TITLE TRANSFER

What this means

This section specifies when responsibility (risk) and ownership (title) of materials shift from you to the client. Typically, risk transfers upon delivery and acceptance, while title transfers after full payment.

Type of company this is important for

Contractors supplying equipment, materials, or prefabricated items, such as suppliers or main contractors on large projects.

Why it's important to negotiate this

By clearly defining when risk and title transfer, you protect yourself from liability for damage or loss after materials are delivered and accepted. This prevents disputes and unexpected costs and ensures both parties understand their responsibilities.

www.ingramcontent.com/pod-product-compliance
Lightning Source LLC
Chambersburg PA
CBHW041301240426
43661CB00010B/984